T0316826

CAMBRIDGE LIBRARY COLLECTION

Books of enduring scholarly value

Archaeology

The discovery of material remains from the recent or the ancient past has always been a source of fascination, but the development of archaeology as an academic discipline which interpreted such finds is relatively recent. It was the work of Winckelmann at Pompeii in the 1760s which first revealed the potential of systematic excavation to scholars and the wider public. Pioneering figures of the nineteenth century such as Schliemann, Layard and Petrie transformed archaeology from a search for ancient artifacts, by means as crude as using gunpowder to break into a tomb, to a science which drew from a wide range of disciplines - ancient languages and literature, geology, chemistry, social history - to increase our understanding of human life and society in the remote past.

The Primeval Antiquities of Denmark

The antiquarian William J. Thoms (1803–85) is probably best remembered today for founding the journal *Notes and Queries* and for having coined the term 'folklore'. He undertook the translation of this work by the Danish archaeologist Jens Worsaae (1821–85) because he felt (as Worsaae says himself) that 'the primeval national antiquities of the British islands have never hitherto been brought into a scientific arrangement'. Believing that this had arisen partly because of the difficulty of distinguishing between some of the many different cultures in Britain's past, Thoms also felt that British interpretations of finds were too frequently beset by 'fanciful theories'. Cultural ties between Britain and Denmark during the Dark Ages meant that finds in Denmark could illuminate British discoveries, and vice versa: Worsaae's work could therefore guide future excavations in Britain. Highly influential and illustrated with woodcuts, this translation first appeared in 1849.

Cambridge University Press has long been a pioneer in the reissuing of out-of-print titles from its own backlist, producing digital reprints of books that are still sought after by scholars and students but could not be reprinted economically using traditional technology. The Cambridge Library Collection extends this activity to a wider range of books which are still of importance to researchers and professionals, either for the source material they contain, or as landmarks in the history of their academic discipline.

Drawing from the world-renowned collections in the Cambridge University Library and other partner libraries, and guided by the advice of experts in each subject area, Cambridge University Press is using state-of-the-art scanning machines in its own Printing House to capture the content of each book selected for inclusion. The files are processed to give a consistently clear, crisp image, and the books finished to the high quality standard for which the Press is recognised around the world. The latest print-on-demand technology ensures that the books will remain available indefinitely, and that orders for single or multiple copies can quickly be supplied.

The Cambridge Library Collection brings back to life books of enduring scholarly value (including out-of-copyright works originally issued by other publishers) across a wide range of disciplines in the humanities and social sciences and in science and technology.

The Primeval Antiquities of Denmark

Translated, and Applied to the Illustration
of Similar Remains in England

J.J.A. WORSAAE
TRANSLATED BY WILLIAM J. THOMS

CAMBRIDGE
UNIVERSITY PRESS

University Printing House, Cambridge, CB2 8BS, United Kingdom

Cambridge University Press is part of the University of Cambridge.
It furthers the University's mission by disseminating knowledge in the pursuit of
education, learning and research at the highest international levels of excellence.

www.cambridge.org
Information on this title: www.cambridge.org/9781108077941

© in this compilation Cambridge University Press 2015

This edition first published 1849
This digitally printed version 2015

ISBN 978-1-108-07794-1 Paperback

THE

PRIMEVAL ANTIQUITIES

OF

DENMARK.

BY

J. J. A. WORSAAE,

A FOREIGN MEMBER OF THE SOCIETY OF ANTIQUARIES OF LONDON, &C., AND A ROYAL COM-
MISSIONER FOR THE PRESERVATION OF THE NATIONAL MONUMENTS OF DENMARK.

TRANSLATED, AND APPLIED TO THE ILLUSTRATION OF
SIMILAR REMAINS IN ENGLAND,

BY

WILLIAM J. THOMS,

A FELLOW OF THE SOCIETY OF ANTIQUARIES, CORRESPONDING MEMBER OF THE SOCIETY
OF ANTIQUARIES OF SCOTLAND, AND SECRETARY OF THE CAMDEN SOCIETY.

ILLUSTRATED WITH NUMEROUS WOODCUTS.

LONDON,
JOHN HENRY PARKER:
AND BROAD-STREET, OXFORD.
M DCCC XLIX.

OXFORD :
PRINTED BY I. SHRIMPTON.

DEDICATED

TO THE

FELLOWS OF THE SOCIETY OF ANTIQUARIES
OF LONDON,

AND

TO THE MEMBERS OF THE VARIOUS ARCHÆOLOGICAL SOCIETIES

OF

GREAT BRITAIN AND IRELAND,

BY

J. J. A. WORSAAE,
WILLIAM J. THOMS.

CONTENTS.

b

PREFACE

THE ENGLISH EDITION,

WRITTEN BY THE AUTHOR.

WHILST the antiquities of Rome, Greece, and Egypt have been carefully examined and systematically described by English writers, the primeval national antiquities of the British islands have never hitherto been brought into a scientific arrangement. The consequence has been that they have neither furnished those results to history, nor excited that interest with the public in general, which they otherwise would have done. This want of systematic arrangement has probably arisen from the circumstance that on the British islands there exist remains of many different people, as the Celts, the Romans, the Saxons, the North-men and the Normans. It is often difficult to distinguish with certainty the antiquities of those different people, and hence the same remains have, by some authors, been called Celtic or Druidical, by others Roman, by others again Danish, &c.

In order to determine with any degree of certainty the differences between the antiquities of different people, and particularly in order to determine what remains are not Roman, it will evidently be serviceable to British antiquaries to look to the national antiquities of countries that were never conquered by the Romans, and whose national remains are therefore unmixed. In that respect the primeval antiquities of Denmark are peculiarly important. Denmark was peopled at a very early age; it lay beyond the pale of Roman conquest; and there the ante-Roman civilization was kept up to a much later period than in the south and west of Europe. The Royal Museum of Northern Antiquities of Copenhagen contains a greater number of primeval antiquities, than most other collections, and by the efforts of C. J. Thomsen, (the real founder of the Museum,) it has been systematically arranged. The close connection which in the old time existed between Denmark and the British islands, renders it natural that British antiquaries should turn with interest to the antiquities of Denmark, and compare them with those of their own countries.

The present little work, which gives a short review of the Danish antiquities compared with the other antiquities of Scandinavia, was originally written in Danish for a Copenhagen society for the diffusion of useful knowledge[a]. It was not my plan to write a book merely for the archæologist, but more particularly for the general reader. I endeavoured to prove the use and importance of archæological researches, by shewing how the early history of our country can be read through the monuments, and I wanted in that way to excite a more general interest for the preservation of our national remains.

In the supposition that this little book would be acceptable to English readers, my friend Mr. Thoms had already, without my knowledge, translated it into English before my arrival in

[a] The Danish title is: "Danmarks Oldtid oplyst ved Oldsager og Grav-höie. Udgivet af Selskabet for Trykkefrihedens rette Brug. Kjöbenhavn, 1843. 8vo. It has also been published in a German translation. "Dänemarks Vorzeit, durch Alterthümer beleuchtet." Kopenhagen, 1844. 8vo.

England, and Mr. Parker had undertaken the publication. But since its publication I have had an opportunity of picking up a good deal of new information by examining the national antiquities of several foreign countries, and last year I published some of the results at which I had recently arrived in another book[b]. Both Mr. Thoms and Mr. Parker agreed with me, that it would be desirable that the English edition should be corrected and enlarged with some of my new observations. I have therefore made a good many alterations, and additions, particularly in the general historical review. I have brought in more information about the connection between the antiquities of our country with those of Germany, Switzerland, France, &c., which, as I hope, will be found to possess some interest. It is only through a comparison of the national antiquities of the different European countries that we shall be enabled to trace the large historical results.

British Archæology has suffered very much from the want of a fixed nomenclature. This has caused a great deal of confusion. The same names and terms have been used for the most different remains. Mr. Thoms and myself have been anxious to give more fixed names. For instance, in the following work the term *cromlech* has only been applied to the monuments of the stone-period; and the name *celt* has not, as before, been given alike to stone hatchets, stone hammers, and to two different sorts of bronze hatchets, but only to one sort of bronze hatchet which is commonly called so on the continent, &c. I think that antiquaries can scarcely pay too much attention to the introduction of a fixed terminology.

[b] Blekingske Mindesmærker fra He-denold. Kjöbenham, 1846. 4to. It has lately appeared in a German trans-lation in "Zur Alterthumskunde des Nordens von J. J. A. Worsaae. Leipzig 1847." 4to.

From the many valuable and interesting notes about similar remains in England, which have been added by Mr.
Thoms from the writings of other antiquaries, it will appear,
that there exists a great similarity between the Danish and
the British antiquities. The same division of the antiquities into three classes,—those belonging to the periods of
Stone, and Bronze, and Iron,—which has been adopted in
the arrangement of the Danish primeval monuments, will
apply to the British remains; and very nearly the same results, in regard to the state of civilization in the stone and
bronze periods, as have been gained for Denmark, will also
be gained for Britain through a careful examination of its
primeval antiquities. At the same time it is perfectly clear,
that the British antiquities, when once sufficiently collected,
examined and compared, will on the whole give more interesting and important results, than have been derived from
those of Denmark, or of most other countries, because they
belong to so many and such different people. I myself in
my travels in Holland, Ireland, and England, have seen how
many most interesting antiquities and monuments still exist
in those countries; and I am fully convinced, that a syste-
matical description and comparison of those remains will throw
quite a new light upon the early state of the British islands,
and particularly that it will present inestimable illustrations on
the civilization and connections of the people from the time of
the Anglo-Saxons until the invasion of the Normans. It is
only through the monuments that we are enabled to trace
the influence of the Roman civilization upon the Celts, until
it was superseded by those new invaders, who laid the foundation of the subsequent progress of England on the ruins
of the Roman civilization. I hope the day is not far distant

when the British people will have formed a national museum of antiquities commensurate with the importance of their remains. It is only in that way that they can be enabled to read the history of their country through its national monuments.

If my book should have a little of the same effect in England, as that which it was intended to produce in Denmark, viz., to excite a more lively interest in the national remains, I think it will do some good. And even in any case,—if it only shews how important it is that the British and Danish antiquaries should unite their efforts more than has hitherto been the case,—I hope the translation will not be regarded as entirely without use. I feel quite sure that such union could not exist without producing most valuable results for the history of both countries.

J. J. A. WORSAAE,
Copenhagen.

PREFACE

BY

THE EDITOR OF THE ENGLISH EDITION.

In the Preface which the reader has just perused, my learned friend Mr. Worsaae has so well described the object of his valuable little work—of which the present must be regarded rather in the light of a new edition than a translation—that any Preface from me, as its English editor, might at first sight appear altogether uncalled for.

In justice to myself however I feel it right to direct the reader's attention to one or two matters in connection with the present publication.

In the first place, I would briefly explain the motives which induced me to undertake the production of an English version of a work, upon a subject so remotely connected with the branch of antiquarian research to which my attention has been more particularly directed; and, as this explanation may, I trust, not only justify me in what I have done, but tempt others to a further examination of the illustrations of our national antiquities which are to be found in the writings of continental antiquaries, I hope I shall not be considered presumptuous if, in the next place, I venture to point out some mines of information which I think calculated to reward those who will take the trouble to explore them.

In the summer of 1845 my attention was accidentally

drawn to the German or second edition of the present work. I had not turned over many of its pages before I felt that the combined knowledge and common sense of the writer had enabled him to produce a more satisfactory book upon a subject involved in very considerable obscurity than it had ever before been my good fortune to meet with. In the belief that it was a book likely to facilitate the enquiries, and to reduce into somewhat of a method the researches, of our English archæologists, in the imperfectly developed field of primeval antiquities, I ventured to recommend it to their attention in a short review which was inserted in the Archæ-ological Journal.

The appearance of that notice having led to the expression of an opinion on the part of many friends, to whose judgment in such matters I could not but defer, that the publication of an English version of Mr. Worsaae's book would be ren-dering good service to the cause of archæological research, and Mr. Parker having consented to undertake the charge of it, such a publication was determined upon.

Other and more important occupations had occurred to delay the progress of the work, when Mr. Worsaae's visit to this country—a visit which will long be remembered with satisfaction by those who had the opportunity of meeting him—secured me the pleasure of his personal acquaintance, and obtained for the work the benefit of such a thorough revisal by himself, together with such copious additions, as to make it almost a new book instead of a new edition. Its value has not, I trust, been diminished by my endeavour, in the notes for which I hold myself responsible, to make the early national antiquities of Denmark and of this country mutually illustrative of each other. And here it may be very properly explained that the great delay which has taken place in the appearance of the present work has partly had its origin in a wish to make it still more complete, by the addition of a copious Appendix pointing out what remains belonging to the Stone, Bronze, and Iron periods respectively have been found in this country, and the localities in which they were discovered; but the difficulty of securing perfect correctness in the returns of such discoveries, and the length of time necessary to authenticate their accuracy, have necessarily led to the postponement of what will form a very essential supplement to the present volume.

If I am right in my anticipation that the strong practical common sense view, which Mr. Worsaae takes of the primeval antiquities of his native country, will be as readily appreciated here, as it has already been on the continent, it is clear that the publication of an English edition of his work will serve to sweep away from among us the last traces of the many fanciful theories connected with those remains which are a reproach to English archæology; and that the stone chambers will no longer be spoken of as the altars on which human victims were immolated, and that stone hatchets will cease to be described as the sacrificial knives with which the heathen priesthood shed the blood of their fellow-creatures.

Nor is this the only benefit likely to result from its publication; which will it is hoped lead our antiquaries to look to the writings of their continental brethren for that illustration of their studies which in the absence of positive knowledge is only to be obtained by a comparison of objects found in these islands with those discovered abroad, and described by foreign archæologists. As an instance how such comparisons may be instituted, let us take the case of the Gristhorpe

find mentioned in the note p. 96 of the following volume:
and which is with one exception, I believe, the only discovery
of the kind known to have taken place in England.

This tumulus was opened in the month of July, 1834,
by Mr. Beswick, the owner of the estate on which it was
situated, and Mr. Alexander of Halifax. At the depth of six
feet from the surface the spades struck against a hard substance which proved to be a quantity of oak branches loosely
laid together; these being removed an immense log of wood,
situated north and south, seven feet long by three broad,
presented itself to the great satisfaction of these antiquaries.
At one end of the log was what was at first supposed to be
a rude figure of a human face, (but this seems very ques-
tionable, as may be judged by the following woodcuts,)

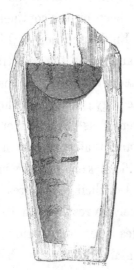 

which circumstance, together with the large size of the log,
led the finders to believe that they had discovered one of the
Druidical remains of the ancient Britons. On attempting
to remove this log on the following morning, it seemed, at

first, to have been broken by the force employed; but on the fractured portion being lifted up, it was found to be the lid of a coffin, the lower part still remaining in the clay, containing a quantity of fluid in which a human skull was visible; and on the water being thrown out it was soon found that the coffin contained a perfect skeleton. The bones were carefully removed, the other contents of the coffin examined, the lower part taken up, and the whole conveyed to the Scarborough Museum, where they are now deposited. The coffin proved to have been made from the trunk of an oak—

Ingentem quercum, decisque undique ramis
Constituit tumulo—

roughly hewn at the extremities, and split with wedges. It had been hollowed by chisels of flint about two inches in width, but must have been cut down with some much larger tool, the marks of its strokes being three inches in length. The outer bottom of the coffin was in length seven feet nine inches, and its extreme breadth three feet three inches. In the bottom, near the centre, is an oblong hole about three inches long by one wide, most probably intended to carry off any fluids arising from the decomposition of the body. There is little difference in size between the lid and body of the coffin. No resin appears to have been used to fix the lid. It was merely loosely laid on, and kept in its place only by the uneven fracture of the wood, the broken portions corresponding on each side when brought into their proper situations.

The skeleton found in the coffin was quite perfect and of an ebony colour[a]. The bones are much larger and stronger

a This remarkable circumstance was thus satisfactorily accounted for by the Dean of Westminster (Dr. Buckland) in a communication addressed by him to the editor of the Literary Gazette. " The extraordinary, and as far as I

than those of a more recent date, exhibiting the lines and
ridges for the attachment of the muscles with a degree of
distinctness rarely if ever witnessed at the present day. But
the most remarkable portion is the head, which is beautifully formed and of extraordinary size. The skeleton, which
has been articulated, measures six feet two inches, and the
interior of the coffin being only five feet four inches accounts
for the disordered state in which the lower extremities were
found, as they must necessarily have been doubled up so as
to admit of being placed within it.

The body, which had been laid on its right side with the
head to the south and its face turned towards the rising sun,
had evidently been wrapped in the skin of some animal, the
hair of which was soft and fine, resembling that of a sheep,
or perhaps more nearly that of a goat, but not quite so long,
and this skin had been originally fastened at the breast with
a pin of horn or bone.

The weapons &c. found in this coffin consist of A. the head
of a spear or javelin, formed of brass or some other composition
of copper; it was much corroded, and had at the broad end
two small rivets used to attach it to a shaft, which from the
shortness of the rivets still remaining must have been broad
and thin.

B. The flint head of a small javelin.

know, unique condition of the bones, preserved by tannin, and converted to the colour of ink, had resulted from the tannin and gallic acid which was in the green oak trunk that forms the coffin, and in its very thick bark. The conversion of the flesh into adipocire must have been occasioned by the ready admission of water through the line of junction of the lid with the body of the coffin, or through the hole cut in the bottom. The clay contained in contact with the body probably contained sufficient iron pyrites to afford the sulphate of iron, which uniting with the tannin and gallic acid, have formed, together with the water within the coffin, an ink of precisely the same materials as that in common use."

C. A beautifully formed ornament of either horn or the bone of some of the larger cetaceous tribe of fishes. The under side is hollowed out to receive some other appendage; and there are three perforations on each side for the purpose of fastening it by means of pins. It had probably been the ornamental head of a javelin, of which the metal head had formed the opposite extremity. Its symmetrical form, which would not disgrace the most expert mechanic of the present day, combined with the gloss upon it, gives it quite a modern appearance.

D. and E. rude arrow-heads of flint.

F. An instrument of wood resembling in form the knife used by the Egyptian embalmers, the point not sharp but round, and flattened on one side to about half its length. The opposite extremity is quite round.

G. A pin of the same material as the ornament of horn or fish. It was laid on the breast of the skeleton, having been used to secure the skin in which the body had been enveloped.

H. Fragments of a ring of horn, composed of two circles connected at two sides. It was of an oval form, too large for the finger, and was probably used for fastening some portion of the dress.

I. By the side of the bones was placed a kind of dish or shallow basket of wicker work, of round form and about six inches in diameter. The bottom had been formed of a single piece of bark, and the side composed of the same, stitched together with the sinews of animals, which, although the basket fell to pieces on exposure to the atmosphere, are still easily to be observed in the fragments and round the edges of the bottom. Attached to the bottom was a quantity of

decomposed matter, the remains, as was supposed, of offerings
of food, either for the dead or as gifts to the gods.

K. Laid upon the lower part of the breast of the skeleton
was a very singular ornament, in the form of a double rose
of riband, with two loose ends. It appeared to have been
an appendage to some belt or girdle, but like the basket, it
fell to pieces immediately on being removed. It is very
uncertain of what it was composed : it was something resembling thin horn, but more opaque and not elastic. The
surface had been simply though curiously ornamented with
small elevated lines.

L. Lastly, a quantity of vegetable substance was also found
in the coffin. It was at first believed to be rushes, and being
afterwards macerated, although the greater portion of it was
so decomposed that nothing but the fibre remained, in one
or two instances the experiment was so far successful as to
distinguish a long lanceolate leaf resembling the misletoe, to
which plant they most probably belonged ; this supposition
was strengthened by the discovery of some few dried berries,
among the vegetable masses, about the size of those of the
misletoe. They were however very tender, and soon crumbled
to dust.

We have remarked that this discovery stands almost alone
in this country. Let us now therefore turn to an account,
unfortunately very imperfect, of a somewhat similar one made
at Bolderup near Haderslev, in 1827, the particulars of
which are recorded in the third volume of the *Nordisk Tidskrift for Oldkyndighed,* published by the Royal Society of
Antiquaries of Copenhagen. The tumulus in which this
primitive coffin was found was celebrated in the traditions of
the neighbourhood. According to some of these it was the

burial-place of a great hero named Bolder or Balder; and according to others, a light was often seen burning on its summit, which was held to be a sure sign that the mound contained hidden treasures. Some excavations had been made by treasure-seekers in 1827, but after digging to the depth of four or five feet without meeting with any thing, further search was abandoned. After this a farmer in the neighbourhood having occasion to fill up some trenches or hollows on his farm, agreed with the proprietor of the mound for permission to cart away so much earth as he wanted, one of the conditions being, that whatever treasure might be found, should be equally divided between the farmer and the proprietor. At about six feet above the level of the surrounding earth, a small urn of baked clay was found, which almost immediately fell to pieces. This gave fresh hopes of finding the expected treasure : the work was continued, and on arriving at the level of the adjacent lands, the workman came to a heap of small granite stones, about the size of a clenched fist, together with one very large one. On removing these, a large shapeless chest presented itself, which was of course immediately looked upon as nothing less than the expected treasure. According to the account of the finder, it was a work of great labour to remove the stones, and while doing so his foot penetrated through the lid of the chest; when finding that it was full of water he dug a trench from it to allow the water to run off.

His next endeavour was to open the chest, and this he accomplished in a very awkward manner, by thrusting a hand-spike into the hole which his foot had made, and so turning over the lid and breaking it off. By this means a quantity of earth fell into the coffin, but not until it had been seen that it contained various objects laid in some degree of order.

Unfortunately no one accustomed to such researches was present, for it was not till some little time afterwards that the news of the discovery reached the Rev. Mr. Prehn, a clergyman in the neighbourhood, to whose care is owing the preservation of the following particulars and the several objects described.

The cist or coffin consisted of a massive oak stem, which had only been roughly hewn and not fashioned into any shape. It exhibited no marks of a saw; and it was obvious that the lid had been formed from the same trunk or stem, in the same way and by the same means. Its extreme length was rather more than ten feet, and the cavity about seven feet long and two broad. At the western part of it there lay in the water (A) a cloak, which took up about half the length, formed of a very peculiar material, being made of several layers of coarse woollen stuff which were sewn together. On the outer edge was sewn a sort of fringe, which consisted of a number of short, fine, black threads, each with a knot at the end. This is altogether very peculiar, and the cloak must have been very thick. Some fragments of it have been preserved in the Museum at Copenhagen. By this cloak there lay (B) some long locks of brown human hair, and by the side of these (C) a bronze sword with a tongue-handle of the same metal; the handle had seemingly been of oak, but it had perished. The sword was of the usual form and size; and the handle had been fastened to it by rivets in a half circle. (D) a dagger also of bronze, the handle which had been fastened to it by rivets was lost. (E) a paalstab of bronze in most excellent preservation, and ornamented on its sides with lines and zigzags. Of the wooden handle which is known to belong to this kind of tool or instrument, there was nothing to be seen. (F) a bronze fibula of the kind commonly found in old grave-hills, the plate being formed of a circular piece of twisted metal, and the pin straight. It is not known in what part of the coffin it lay originally, as it was not seen at first. It is asserted that there was also found at the western end of the coffin, by the side of the locks of hair already mentioned, a comb, resembling in its general appearance those usually found in the northern grave-hills, but what is extremely unusual, it is of horn. It is ornamented with perforations and flame-like incisions. At the eastern end of the coffin a vessel of wood was discovered, which fell to pieces as it was being lifted out of the water with a spade, but in which nothing was found upon a subsequent examination except that there appeared something which looked like ashes on the bottom of it. This vessel was round, about a foot in diameter, and had two ears on the sides. It is somewhat remarkable that this oak trunk, which had been so hollowed out that it would readily have held the body of a full-grown man, should not, apparently, have contained any traces of a human skeleton. But looking to the parties by whom it was discovered, and the peculiar notions they have upon such matters, it is suspected the remains had been removed and secretly interred again, probably in some churchyard[b].

Nor is this Danish account of the discovery of an interment in a tree coffin, the only one which exists to illustrate the Gristhorpe find. For it appears by two passages in the recently published *Geschichte der Deutschen Sprache*, by Jacob Grimm, that there has lately been a remarkable find at Lupfen near Oberflacht in Suabia, of the so-called *Todten-*

---

[b] Nordisk Tidskrift for Oldkyndighed udgivet af det Kongelike Nordiske Oldskrift-Selskab. Bd. III. o. 279.

bäume, that is to say, of stems of oaks which have been hollowed out for the purpose of being used as coffins, and which he says not improbably belonged to the times of Ala-mannic heathendom, possibly to as early a period as the fourth century. The particulars of this discovery have been made known by the Wurtemburg Antiquarian Society, but unfortunately I have not succeeded in obtaining a sight of the book in which they are recorded. This I the more regret, as it is obvious from the mention which Grimm makes of the various articles of wood found at the same time, such as the death-shoes, (the German *Todten Schuh,* the *Helskó* of the old Norse-men,) the symbolical wooden hands, and a musical instrument somewhat resembling a violin, that this discovery is calculated to throw great light upon ancient funereal rites[c], and upon the mythology on which those rites were founded.

[c] The following extract from the article 'Madagascar' in the Encyclo-pædia Metropolitana, is so curiously illustrative of the present subject, that I cannot refrain from adding it in the shape of a note. "Their funeral rites have a considerable resemblance to those of the Bechwána tribes on the opposite coast of Africa. The nearest relations assemble at the house of the deceased, the men with their heads and beards shorn, the women wearing a cap as a sign of mourning. The corpse is richly ornamented with rings, chains, coral, &c., and wrapped up in its finest clothes. The women dance and bewail alternately, the men perform feats of arms. Others, in an adjoining room, extol the deceased, ask why he died? Whether he had not gold, cattle, slaves enough? And in this wild alternation of lamentation and feasting, the first day of mourning is past. A tree is then cut down for the coffin, hollowed out, sprinkled with the blood of a slaughtered ox or cow, consecrated by prayer, and finally carried, the corpse having been enclosed in it, by six relations of the deceased, to the family burial-place, (amunúkŏ,) and deposited outside of the enclosure surrounding it. A fire is made at each corner of the burying-ground, frankincense is sprinkled upon the embers, the head of the family, standing at the gate calls aloud upon each of his ancestors by name, and entreats them to entertain the new comer well; after which the grave is dug, and the corpse interred without further ceremony. In fifteen days' time more sacrifices are made, provisions are placed near the grave, and the heads of the victims are stuck on poles round the tomb."

The reader need scarcely be reminded that these death-shoes were laid by the side of the corpse on account of a popular superstition formerly very prevalent, of one form of which Aubrey has left us a curious record in the remarkable Yorkshire dirge so frequently printed[d]. He tells us that this superstition had its origin in the belief which obtained of the souls of the dead "having to pass through a great lande full of thornes and furzen;" and also that the custom of burying the dead in coffins, formed from the hollowed trunks of trees, and shaped like the boats or canoes they had been wont to use, sprung from a belief that in their passage to the realms of immortality the souls of the departed had to cross the waters which divided the world of the living from that of the dead[e].

In the belief that the one instance I have given will serve as well as twenty to prove the position I have advanced, namely, that great results may be looked for from our English archæologists consulting the writings of their fellow labourers on the continent, I will content myself with pointing out some few works which have come under my own observation, and seem to me deserving the attention of those who take an interest in the study of primeval antiquities.

Klemm's Handbuch der Germanischen Altherthumskunde[f] is a small octavo volume, rendered both useful and interesting from its numerous illustrations, and the abundant references in the foot notes to the writings of German antiquaries on every branch of the early antiquities of their country.

More peculiarly local in its specific object, but very useful

---

[d] Scott's Minstrelsy ; Ellis's edition of Brand's Antiquities ; and in my " Anecdotes and Traditions."

[e] For much illustration of these curious points in popular mythology, see Grimm's Deutsche Mythologie, (ed. 1844,) p. 190 et seq.

[f] Dresden, 1836.

and valuable from the minuteness of its details, and its faith-
ful illustrations of objects, is the *Heidnische Altherthumer der
Gegend von Uelzen im chemaligen Bardengaue (Konigreich
Hanover) von G. O. Carl von Estorff*[g].

Our Celtic antiquaries too would do well to consult the
*Taschenbuch fur Geschichte und Altherthum in Süddeutsch-
land*, edited by Dr. *Heinrich Schreiber*, of which five volumes
have appeared, the first being published at Freiburg in 1839.
Dr. Schreiber's learned Essay on the Torc of the Celts, one of
many equally valuable papers, would alone satisfy the reader
of the great value of this antiquary's labours.

But far more important than any of the works I have
mentioned are Mr. Worsaae's own later contributions to
archæological science, of which a list will be found in the
subjoined note[h], inasmuch as they contain a fuller development of this accomplished scholar's views than is to be found
in the present elementary book.

Nor need the English antiquary confine himself in his search
for illustrations of English primeval antiquities to continental
authorities alone.　For much that is highly curious and valu-

---

[g] Hanover, 1846.

[h] 1. *Runamo og Braavalleslaget*. Et
Bidrag sil archæologisk Kritik ap
J. J. A. Worsaae.　Kjöbenhavn (Co-
penhagen), 1844. 4to.　Med et Tillæg.
Kjöbenhavn 1845. og 5 Tavler.

2. *Blekingske Mindesmærker fra
Hedenold* betragtede i deres Forhold
til de örrige skandinaviske og europæ-
iske Oldtidsminder af J. J. A. Worsaae.　Med 15 lith. Tavler.　Kjöbenhavn 1846. 4to.

No. 1 and 2 also translated into
German in:
Zur Alterthumskunde des Nordens
von J. J. A. W.　Leipzig 1847. 4to.

mih 20 Tafeln.

3. *Die nationale Alterthumskunde
in Deutschland*.　Reisebemerkungen
von J. J. A. W.　Aus dem Dänischen.
Kopenhagen 1846. 8vo. Leipzig bei
Rudolph Hartmann.

4. *Danevirke, Danskhedens aldgamle
Grændsevold mod Syden* ap J. J. A. W.
Kjöbenhavn 1848.　8vo.

Translated into German:
*Danevirke, der alte Gränzwall Däne-
marks gejen Süden*, ein geschichtlicher
Beitrag zur wahren Auffassung der
Schleswigschen Frage, von J. J. A. W.
Kopenhagen 1848. 8vo. Verlag von
C. A. Reitzel.

able will be found in a handsome quarto volume, published last year by the Smithsonian Institution of Washington, under the title *Ancient Monuments of the Missisippi Valley, by E. G. Squire, M.A. and E. H. Davis, M.D.*, a volume strikingly illustrative of the uniformity which exists between the primitive implements of all the varieties of the human race.

Before concluding. this Preface, the Editor cannot refuse himself the pleasure of alluding to two valuable contributions towards a more correct knowledge of our early antiquities, which have appeared since he undertook the task of giving an English version of Mr. Worsaae's work.   The first of them is Mr. Akerman's very useful *Archæological Index to Remains of Antiquity of the Celtic, Romano-British, and Anglo-Saxon Periods*, with its numerous and characteristic illustrations; and the second, the *Guide to Northern Archæology, by the Royal Society of Northern Antiquaries of Copenhagen, edited for the use of English Readers by the Right Honourable the Earl of Ellesmere*, a volume which may to a certain extent be regarded as a companion to the present hand-book.   Both works are eminently calculated to establish those more precise and accurate views respecting Primeval Antiquities, which it has been Mr. Worsaae's especial object to promote in the little work which I now submit to the candid consideration of the reader.

WILLIAM J. THOMS.

25, HOLY-WELL STREET, MILLBANK, WESTMINSTER,
AUGUST 11TH, 1849.

Stone Hatchet . .

Hollow Chisel . . .

Narrow Chisel . . . .

Knife . . . . . .

Arrow-heads . . . . .

Paalstab . . . . . .

Celt . . . .

Armlet . .

SPIRAL ORNAMENT . . . .

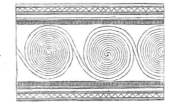

DOUBLE SPIRAL ORNAMENT

RING ORNAMENT . . . . .

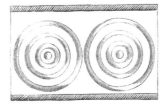

WAVE ORNAMENT . . . .

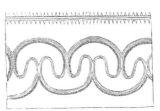

CIRCULAR CROMLECH

LONG CROMLECH

STONE CHAMBER. . . . . .

GIANT'S
CHAMBER } . . . . .

SHIP BARROW . . . . . .

BAUTA STONE . . . . . .

INTRODUCTION.

A NATION which respects itself and its independence cannot possibly rest satisfied with the consideration of its present situation alone. It must of necessity direct its attention to bygone times, with the view of enquiring to what original stock it belongs, in what relations it stands to other nations, whether it has inhabited the country from primeval times or immigrated thither at a later period, to what fate it has been exposed; so as to ascertain by what means it has arrived at its present character and condition. For it is not until these facts are thoroughly understood, that the people acquire a clear perception of their own character, that they are in a situation to defend their independence with energy, and to labour with success at the progressive development, and thus to promote the honour and well-being of their country. At all times, therefore, has history, which describes the early state of nations, occupied a distinguished place in the scale of philosophical enquiry; at all times has the endeavour to explain and illustrate history been in the same proportion honoured and esteemed. It is thus evident that with us Danes, as well as with other races, it must be an object to obtain, as far as possible, a thorough knowledge of the immigration, origin, manners, customs, and achievements of our forefathers. This knowledge

B

is to us doubly desirable and necessary, since all historical
records combine to shew us that our ancestors, during the
period of pagan antiquity, played a very important part among
European nations; while, moreover, it cannot be denied that
we are better able to ascertain the peculiarities of a nation on
its first appearance in history, while it is still unmixed with
others, than to trace them in its modern history, where the
connection with other countries has often visibly exerted such
an influence over the people as to render the task of describing
their national characteristics difficult and uncertain. It is
equally natural that we should wish to know whether any people inhabited this country prior to our ancestors, and what
degree of civilization they possessed. It is of great assistance
to history, to become acquainted with the race or races of people with whom our ancestors came in contact on their immigration into the country; and it may well be supposed that a
review of the oldest form and character, and the earliest occupation of our country, will be welcome to every one who sin-
cerely loves his home.

If we now consider the most ancient accounts of Denmark
and its inhabitants, we shall find that they are enveloped in
obscurity and darkness. We know that the Gothic race who
now occupy this land, and who are nearly allied to the inhabitants of Norway and Sweden, were not the aboriginal
inhabitants of the country. The ancient traditions and songs
speak obscurely of several immigrations, and inform us how
our forefathers and the other Scandinavian Goths, on their
arrival in the North, met with earlier inhabitants, whom they
were compelled either to assimilate with themselves, or to
endeavour to overcome by long and arduous conflicts. But
who these people were, to what degree of civilization they

had attained, how far their rule extended, and whether the whole of the North was then inhabited by one and the same people, are questions which have never yet been answered in a manner satisfactory to history. It is in the writers of Greece and Rome that we find the earliest information respecting our native North; but since these are on the one hand derived from the oral, and often exaggerated and disfigured relations of others, and on the other are brief and imperfect, they are far from affording us any clear idea of the habitations, mode of life, and mutual relations of these various ancient races. Nor are our early northern songs and traditions satisfactory in this respect. They frequently indicate that here in the North, on the immigration of our ancestors, there existed Jetten, or beings of supernatural size, who could with the greatest ease wield enormous rocks; together with dwarfs, (or Svartalfer,) who were small and black, and dwelt in caves under ground; and finally the elves, (Lysalfer,) a handsome, and as it appears, a civilized people, with whom our forefathers are said to have lived in friendly relations. Now, in the opinion of many persons, it is sufficiently certain that under these names and descriptions various races of people are intended; but it is no less clear that it is only with the greatest caution, and even then with considerable uncertainty, that we can appeal to these and similar accounts, when it is our object to deduce from them historical information of a satisfactory kind. For we must remember that such traditions were not recorded till they had been for centuries handed down from generation to generation; and thus it may easily be conceived how, in such oft-repeated traditions, something has often been added or taken away, so that the original historical fact which forms the basis of the tradition or song, has frequently, we may in fact say in almost every instance, become altered beyond the power of recognition. Even at the present day we have frequent instances of the same events being described in a very different manner, even in print; how much more easily then could such be the case, in times when intercourse between distant countries was far less frequent, and when it must naturally have been extremely difficult to ascertain the truth or falsehood of any statement. It is besides more than probable that many traditions referring to pagan times, which were not recorded till more than a hundred years after the introduction of Christianity, are mingled more or less with Christian additions.

For the same reason it must also be confessed that we know but little that is certain, as to the earliest condition of the present inhabitants of Denmark, or of our predecessors in this country, although there is no want of narratives on the subject. With the diffusion of Christianity, or about the period of Gorm the Old, who lived in the first half of the tenth century, our history begins to be somewhat more trustworthy, although it is still dark and incomplete. Almost every thing previous to that date (the year 900) is merely preserved in traditions and statements, in which it is extremely difficult to distinguish the false from the true. Even the state of civilization attained by our forefathers is a point upon which we are by no means fully informed. Endeavours have meantime been made to remedy this imperfect state of things, and recourse has been had to the records of Sweden and Norway, and from these documents conclusions have been drawn as to what took place in Denmark. It will, however, readily be perceived that such attempts must be attended with very unsatisfactory results. For even if the Danes, Swedes, and Norwegians lived in close connection with each other, yet such a circumstance by no means proves that they possessed the same institutions, manners, and customs. In particular, the different conditions of _nature and of climate of the several countries of Scandinavia must have produced numerous, and by no means unimportant differences among the inhabitants, a supposition which is confirmed by numerous facts.

But it may be asked, how can we then ever hope to arrive, in some degree, at a clear knowledge of the early history of our native land. Such a result, as we have already shewn, can be effected only in part, by means of the existing records. It becomes therefore necessary to look to other sources, from which we may not only derive fresh facts, but also obtain confirmation and illustration of those facts which are preserved in our early records. Recognising this principle, attention has recently been directed to the indisputable memorials of antiquity which we possess in the Cromlechs, Cairns, Barrows or Grave-hills, Stone-circles, &c., which lie scattered over the country, as well as in the many and diversified objects of antiquarian interest which have been discovered in them. It was a well-founded supposition, that by the examination and comparison of these, we should probably, at least in part, discover the wished-for explanations, while it is of course obvious that these actual remains of the olden times are incapable of being modified in the course of years in the same manner as oral traditions.

We now proceed to the enquiry how far this opinion has been confirmed by modern investigation. With the view of rendering our statements as clear and intelligible as possible,

we shall deem it most expedient first to investigate those antiquities which have been exhumed from the earth.   This will
be followed by the description of the existing monuments,
the Standing Stones—and those with Runic inscriptions,
and we shall then conclude with a general review of the
whole subject.

FIRST DIVISION.

As collections of antiquities were intended to afford illustrations of history, it followed as a natural consequence, that as soon as a few objects were collected, attempts were made to explain them. The course which was at first pursued was, however, obviously incorrect: for example, it was at once perceived that the antiquities which had been discovered differed materially from each other, since some were carved from stone, while others were beautifully formed of metal. Although it was now generally acknowledged that our native land had been inhabited by several distinct races, still it was supposed that all these antiquities must have belonged to one and the same people, namely, those who were the last that found their way into our country, the Goths of Scandinavia, from whom we derive our descent. By this means, objects appertaining to the most different times were naturally mingled together. We will quote a striking instance of this fact, and we do so because the view which is here maintained is one which is still not unfrequently expressed both in writing and in conversation.

It is well known that stones shaped by art into the form of wedges, hammers, chisels, knives, &c., are frequently exhumed from the earth. These, in the opinion of many, could certainly never have served as tools or implements, since it was impossible either to carve or cut with a stone; hence it was concluded, that they had formerly been employed by our forefathers in those sacrifices which were offered to idols, during the prevalence of heathenism. Thus it was said the hammers of stone were used to strike the sacrifice on the forehead; and after the sacrificing priest with a chisel, likewise formed of stone, had stripped off the skin, the flesh was cut to pieces with knives of stone, &c. The Cromlechs,

Cairns, and Barrows in which such objects are found, were conceived to have been partly places of sacrifice, partly temples and seats of justice. But when amidst the vast mass of antiquities of stone which had been gradually collected, several shewed obvious marks of having been much used and worn, doubts began to be entertained whether they really had been employed as instruments of sacrifice. At length attention was directed to the fact that even at the present day, in several of the islands of the South seas and in other parts, there exist races of savages who, without knowing the use of metals, employ implements of stone which have the same shape and adaptation as those which are discovered in the earth in such quantities in Denmark, and further, it was shewn in what manner those savages made use of such simple and apparently such useless implements. No one after this could longer remain in doubt that our antiquities of stone were also actually used as tools in times when metals were either unknown, or were so rare and costly, that they were only in the possession of very few individuals. That this could not have been the case in this country while inhabited by our forefathers the Goths, is evident from all historical records, we must therefore seek for the origin of the antiquities of stone in an earlier time, in fact, as we shall soon perceive, among the first inhabitants of our native land.

As soon as it was once pointed out that the whole of these antiquities could by no means be referred to one and the same period, people began to see more clearly the difference between them. We are now enabled to pronounce with certainty, that our antiquities belonging to the times of paganism may be referred to three chief classes, referable to three distinct periods. The first class includes all antiquarian objects formed of stone, respecting which we must assume that they appertain to the stone-period, as it is called, that is, to a period when the use of metals was in a great measure unknown. The second class comprises the oldest metallic objects; these however were not as yet composed of iron, but of a peculiar mixture of metals, copper and a small portion of tin melted together, to which the name of "bronze" has been given; from which circumstance the period in which this substance was commonly used has been named the bronze-period. Finally, all objects appertaining to the period when iron was generally known and employed, are included in the third class, and belong to the iron-period.

We will now consider these three classes, each by itself, and will commence naturally with the most ancient, the so called stone-period.

I. Antiquities of the Stone-period.

Denmark seems to have been raised by a powerful revolution of nature from the bosom of the sea. By degrees its naked banks of gravel became covered with aspen forests. When the land rose still higher and the dampness diminished, the aspen disappeared after having by numerous successive growths formed a way for the fir, which now spread all over the country. This species of tree continued for a very long period, but at length was compelled to give place to a very different and a higher class. At first the beech was unable to grow here. The earth was covered with oaks, of that species termed the winter oak, which differs from the now prevailing species, the summer oak; these were succeeded by groves of alders, until all was so prepared and developed that the light and beautiful beech spread its crowns over the whole country.

That Denmark in its primeval times, before it possessed its present vegetation, had passed through these four periods, is clearly proved from the ancient peat bogs, in which are found stems of trees of each distinct period lying like beds one over the other. As they are usually found lying in a prostrate position, many have supposed that the changes in vegetation have been caused by powerful and mighty phenomena in nature, such as storms and floods. This idea however is by no means probable. It is much more likely that the trees have fallen down from time to time in the bog, and that the different changes are but the result of the ordinary progressions of nature. With peculiar kinds of wood peculiar plants and animals must have been associated. At a period when the country was covered with forests of oak, in all probability there lived animals that are now extinct, such as the reindeer, the elk and the aurochs, the horns and bones of all which are frequently found. It is not improbable that these animals existed to a much later period in these forests, and that they were only exterminated by the slings, the weapons, and the traps of the inhabitants[a].

If we now enquire, whether Denmark was inhabited by men in any one of the four periods which preceded the present beech vegetation, the answer we obtain is very indefinite. The most ancient historical accounts which testify that Denmark was entirely overgrown with forests, nowhere mention that these forests consisted of any other trees than the beech. If we consider that the beech has existed here from two to three thousand years, and that each of the four other classes of trees may have required the same time for their growth and disappearance, it will unquestionably appear somewhat hazardous to refer the peopling of Denmark either to the period of the alder, or that of the oak, each of which periods dates from some thousands of years. We must, however, observe that we are here discussing the question of a period respecting which we have no certain information. It is therefore very possible that Denmark may have been inhabited prior to the vegetation of the beech.

Thus much, however, appears under all circumstances to be certain, that when the first inhabitants came to Denmark, which may have been at least three thousand years ago, they found a country covered with a continued range of enormous forests. In the interior these were almost impassable; but their density and thickness diminished as they approached the

[a] According to J. Steenstrup.

coast. The coast itself was probably quite devoid of wood: it therefore followed, as a matter of course, that the new comers would fix their dwellings in that quarter.

As the country was then rude and waste, so the first inhabitants also were rude and uncultivated in the highest degree. They did not commonly possess a knowledge of copper, of iron, or of any metals: they formed all their implements and weapons of wood, of the bones of animals, or of stone. As stone is not subject to be destroyed by being deposited in the earth, numerous instruments have been preserved to our own time, from which we can form some idea of the degree of civilization attained by the inhabitants of our native land at that period.

One of the most useful tools, for felling trees, for forming houses, and for executing works in wood generally, was the hatchet. Their hatchets were nearly in the form of the wedges now in use, but somewhat broader, and had no regular neck. Their sizes were very various; they are found from three to fifteen inches in length, and from one to four inches in breadth[b]. With the view to their being as useful as possible, they were formed of the hardest kinds of stone, and in Denmark almost exclusively of flint. They were first rudely struck out, and were then polished. The polishing, however, is by no means alike in every part; some are found polished on all their sides, some on the two broad sides, and some merely at the edge. The edge itself was usually very sharp, yet still of tolerable thickness, which made the hatchet both stronger and more useful for working in

[b] The following engraving of a hatchet six inches and a half in length, exhibits a form which is very commonly found both in England and Ireland.—T.

wood. The hatchet was originally fixed to a wooden handle, but since wood, as is well known, is decomposed by lying in the ground, no such handle has hitherto been discovered in Denmark[c]. We have, however, good grounds for supposing that the hatchet was provided with a handle, in the same manner as similar stone hatchets which are used by savage nations now existing. It was fastened either to a straight or to a crooked handle. The crooked handle was partly divided, as is seen in the hatchet figured here, which is from an island in the South Sea, so that the stone was placed in the opening, and there fastened, either with the fibres of plants or the intestines of animals. By this means this advantage was gained, that the longer the hatchet was used the stronger the stone was imbedded in its position. In some cases the handle was furnished with an incision or notch, so that by binding the upper part of the hatchet to the wood

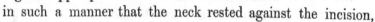

in such a manner that the neck rested against the incision,

as here, (a at 1,) the inconvenience of the hatchet slipping from its fastenings, and so falling out, was avoided. The handle was often split, but it being difficult to hold the axe firmly in such a handle, we see (at 2) that the savage people who still use such handles often cover the stone with pitch, and compress the handle round it by means of thongs and ties. In this, or at least in some similar manner, in all probabi-

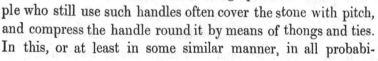

[c] Though no such handle has been found in Denmark, a specimen was discovered some years since near Cookstown in the county of Tyrone, and was, when seen by Mr. Du Noyer, who has described it in his Paper on the Classification of Celts, (Archæological Journal, vol. iv. p. 3,) in the possession of Colonel Stewart of Killymoon.—T.

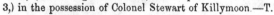

lity, those of our stone hatchets were fastened which have a bent and polished edge.

The most ancient inhabitants, or as we may term them, the aborigines, would have made but little progress, had they attempted to fell a large and full-grown tree, with nothing more than so imperfect an instrument as the stone hatchet. They doubtless pursued the same method as the savages of our days, who when about to fell a tree with stone hatchets, avail themselves also of the assistance of fire, in the following manner. In the first place some of the bark is peeled off, by means of the hatchet, from the tree which is to be felled. In the opening thus made coals are placed, which are fanned till they are all consumed. By this means a portion of the stem is charred, which is then hewn away with the hatchet, and fresh coals are continually added until the tree is burned through. In our peat bogs old stems of trees have been found which appear to have been thus felled by stone hatchets with the aid of fire.

It can scarcely be doubted that their boats must have been of a very simple kind. From several relics which have been dug up[d], we may conclude that the aborigines in the

[d] A curious boat of this description was found in a bog in the barony of Farney. It was formed of the hollowed trunk of an oak tree, and measured twelve feet in length, and three feet in breadth, and, as will be seen by the accompanying engraving, derived from Mr. E. P. Shirley's interesting 'Account of the Barony of Farney,' was furnished with handles at the extremities, evi-

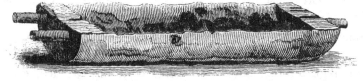

dently for facility of transport from one lough to another, in a country where so large a portion of the surface was covered by water. In the Archæologia (vol. xxvi. p. 264) will be found an engraving and description of an ancient canoe found at North Stoke in Sussex, and now in the British Museum. It is no less than 35 feet in length, and is formed of one half of a large oak tree cut off square at the ends and hollowed. In the description of the North Stoke canoe will be found references to various similar boats found in this country; and we read in it, that "Beverley, in his account of Virginia p. 198. says he had seen a canoe made by the Indians of a tree hollowed by fire, and cut and scraped by their *stone tomahawks*, 30 feet long."—T.

usual manner of savage nations, charred the stem of the
tree at the root and the summit only, and then hollowed it
out by means of fire till it acquired its equilibrium on the
water. To this use the instruments which have been termed
hollow chisels, (1) were most probably destined. These like
the hatchets are formed of flint, and only differ from them in
the fact of their edges being always ground hollow in a

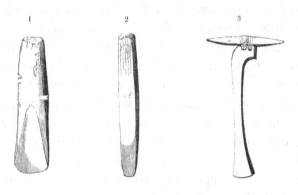

very careful manner.   Among the implements of this age we
must also reckon some small long four-cornered pieces of
stone (2) which have been named narrow chisels. They are
always formed of flint, are from three to eleven inches long,
have a sharp edge, and appear to have been fastened by
moistened thongs to wooden handles, as in figure (3), which
is a drawing of a similar implement from the South Sea. The
knives, both those used for domestic purposes and those employed in works of labour, are of flint, two edged and with a
broad blade, and frequently have handles hollowed out of the
stone itself. Not unfrequently these handles are adorned
with regular ornaments; at other times, they are less carefully formed, as if they
had been destined to be
enveloped or inserted in
wood. These knives are
usually from three to
twelve inches in length. They are scarcely ever polished,

probably because the edge is so thin that in most cases it would have broken to pieces in polishing. There are also crooked half-moon shaped knives of flint, which are occasionally provided with saw-like teeth, on which account they are named saw-blades.

In addition to these implements, which were inserted into wooden handles, the aborigines had others which were bored with regular holes for handles, that is, mauls or hammers[e], among which those which have perforations close to the neck are commonly called axes[f]. They are not formed of

[e] The subjoined representation, (taken from Mr. E. P. Shirley's " Account of the Territory or Dominion of Farney,") reduced to one half the original size, exhibits a very interesting specimen of one of these hammer-heads, found in a bog near the banks of Lough Fee, in Ireland. It is of hornstone, and is remarkable on account of its peculiar form, and the skill and precision with which so hard a substance has been fashioned and polished.—T.

[f] The accompanying engraving represents a stone maul or hammer of rather unusual form, found at Llanmadock in Gower, now preserved in

the Museum of the Royal Institution at Swansea, and exhibited at a Meeting of the Archæological Institute by Mr. George Grant Francis. Its length is 6 in. and its weight 23 oz.—T.

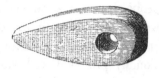

flint but of softer kinds of stone,
particularly trap, which is heavier
and less brittle than flint. The
boring of the hole for the handle
appears, in the most ancient period,
to have been executed in a very
simple manner, perhaps only with a
pointed stick and sand and water;
the hole being bored first on one
side, then on the other, and lastly
broken through the middle. In length they vary from two
to three inches up to twelve. It has been supposed, and
not without reason, that the most simple of them, those
which have the back rounded off or flat, were used as wedges
for splitting trees, in which case they were struck with
wooden mallets. At the same time, like the more neatly
formed hammers, they might have served both for domestic
purposes, and in case of need as maces or battle-axes. Nor
must we forget to mention here, that in several instances
hammers of bone have been found in the earth, in particular
those formed of the antlers of the deer, which at one end
are bored for the handle, at the other are sharpened for
cutting; affording a proof that, in the absence of metals
the aborigines availed themselves of other materials, beside
stone.

If we form a clear conception of what is meant by being
unacquainted with implements of metal, and being compelled
to make use of simple and very imperfect instruments of stone,
such as have been described; and if we remember, at the same
time, that Denmark was at the period referred to, a rude uncultivated and woody country, it is easy to perceive, that the
aborigines could scarcely have paid any particular attention
to agriculture. For though the woods might be extirpated by
means of fire, and it may be assumed that several of the stone
hatchets, placed crosswise in crooked handles of wood, might
possibly have been employed for digging the ground, yet it

is clear that to render the land productive, larger and better implements were necessary than those then existing. On the other hand the conditions of nature pointed out hunting and fishing as the easiest and most available means of subsistence. The forests afforded game, and the waters fish, in abundance; while their habitations on the coast enabled the people to hunt in the woods, or fish in the waters, with equal facility.

Proofs that they actually followed such a mode of life are afforded by the implements for fishing and hunting, formed of stone and bone, which are constantly discovered in the earth. Among the weapons of the chase the arrow-heads are particularly distinguished. They are often of flint, a few inches long, and sometimes triangular or flat, sometimes heart-shaped, which last as a rule are formed with such care that the sides are very finely notched. One peculiar kind of arrows consists of small pieces of bone, in which splinters of flint are inserted. The splinters are universally thin and small, and are fastened by a kind of cement into indentations which are cut in the sides. From the manner in which stone arrow-heads are used in certain countries at the present day, we may conclude that those of Denmark were fastened

to the end of reeds, or fine slips of wood. They were then shot from a bow, that is, a stout branch of a tree, bent by a string fastened to each end of it. These bows have not hitherto been found in the North, for having been formed of wood, they have in the course of time gradually perished from lying in the earth. With these rude weapons for shooting it might be supposed that it was scarcely possible to take any effectual aim.   But it is a fact that the people who, at the present day, make use of bows and arrows of this simple kind, exhibit extraordinary skill in shooting with them.   They hit a bird on the wing with the greatest ease, even at a considerable distance ; and there are even examples, for instance in Brazil, where the marksman throws himself on his back, presses his bow with his feet, and even in that position strikes his prey.   Against birds and other small creatures these stone arrows might prove effectual, but against larger animals such as the aurochs[g], the elk, the reindeer, the stag, and the wild boar, they were evidently insufficient ; particularly since those animals often become furious as soon as they are struck.   The hunters, therefore, in their expeditions for the chase appear to have been provided, not only with a hunting-knife, or dagger like that figured above, (p. 14,) but also with a lance fastened in a long wooden handle.   This was formed of flint, nearly of the same shape as the knife, except that it had no

regular grip, but ran tapering towards the end so as to be fastened into the handle.

The implements used for ca ching fish, exhibit from the circumstance of their handles having perished, so much resemblance to the weapons of the chase, that it is almost impossible to draw an exact line between them.   Thus, for instance, the harpoons were doubtless of precisely the same form as the arrow-heads. As was the case at an earlier period among the inhabitants of Greenland, they certainly were fastened into a handle of wood or of bone; and at the end

[g] The aurochs which has been already mentioned, (p. 10,) is the bison of Europe, whose range is now confined to the forests of Lithuania. A living specimen of this rare animal has recently arrived at the Zoological Gardens. The bones of an aurochs lately furnished the subject of interesting remark at the British Association, to Sir R. Murchison and his brother naturalists.—T.

was bored a hole, into which a longer stick was inserted for the purpose of enabling the harpooner to dart the instrument with greater force against the fish. The harpoons, however, were thrown, not so much for the purpose of killing the fish, as with the view of impeding its course, and so seizing it the more easily. To kill the fish they availed themselves of lances, similar to those employed in the chase. That, from the earliest times, it was the practice to catch fish by means of hooks is seen from the circumstance that such implements formed of flint are occasionally dug up. Similar objects formed of bone, are still used in remote islands. Stones, too, have often been found which appear to have been used to sink fishing-lines. Some are round, with a groove round the middle, some flat and perforated. It is possible that the use of the fishing-net, though of an imperfect form, may then have been known, in which case these stones may have been very useful.

From the mode of life pursued by these aborigines, it is scarcely to be doubted that their apparel consisted chiefly of the skins of such wild beasts as they slew in the chase. This idea is confirmed by the circumstance that bodies clad in such skins have, from time to time, been dug up in our peat bogs. These skins were sewn together in the most simple manner, without any thread, merely with strips of skin. With some of them were also found shoes, which consisted only of a single piece of hide sewn together behind, and fastened to the foot by thongs. If we admit that it is possible that the greater part of these relics belonged to a later period, since remains of woollen cloth have been discovered with them, yet we may conclude with probability from their style, that clothes of skins were not less universal at an earlier and ruder period.

As to any beautiful or costly ornaments, these are entirely out of the question, so long as the materials in use consisted only of stone, bone, wood, or amber, while the tools with which they were to be wrought were chiefly formed of flint.

Their trinkets appear to have consisted partly of great round perforated knobs, or buttons, intended to hold their clothes together over the breast, and partly of beads. These last were chiefly made of amber, since this substance was found on the coasts, possibly in greater quantities than is the case at present. The beads were either shaped in the form of hammers and axes, or rounded off nearly like those now in use, or, more particularly the larger ones, were quite rough and unshaped, and merely perforated. The largest pieces of amber being doubtless the most valuable, their possessors were probably desirous not to diminish their value by rounding or polishing them. Several were occasionally slung toge-

ther and worn round the neck, in such a manner as to reach down to the breast.

Beads and ornaments formed of the bones of animals were also worn in the same way.

We have seen how the aborigines lived and laboured: let us now briefly consider in what way they interred their dead. The bodies were not burned, but placed in chambers which were formed of large flat stones within elevated mounds or barrows, together with the implements, weapons, and ornaments which the deceased when alive had most frequently used. The bodies were also occasionally deposited in vessels of burnt clay. These were in general filled with fine loose earth, but in some cases they appear to have contained provisions placed there in order that the deceased might not feel hunger during their journey to the other world. The largest earthen vessels, it is supposed, were originally made for cooking; what may have been the purpose of the smaller and more finely wrought specimens, which are only found in the tombs appertaining to the stone-period, is uncertain. They are for the most part only a few inches high, and are not formed for

standing upright, but have, near the mouth, small holes or
handles by which they were probably suspended.

Lastly, in the graves, scattered bones, among others those
of the stag, elk, wild boar, dog, and often the teeth of horses,
have been found, but it does not appear to have been the
practice to bury any of these animals, except perhaps occasionally the dog, with the deceased. By this means we learn
that, during this period, domesticated animals, dogs and
horses at all events, existed in Denmark.

Objects of stone very similar to these which we have described in this portion of our work, are found in the North,
out of Denmark, most frequently in the south of Sweden,
while they very rarely occur in Norway or the north of
Sweden. They are also met with along the southern coast
of the Baltic, in Hanover, Holland, England, Scotland, Ireland, and in several places in France, Spain, and Portugal.

It is probable also that there has been a period in which
civilization had attained a higher point in these countries than
it had in Denmark. It would appear that objects of stone
occur more rarely in the south and east of Europe, but upon
this point further information is to be desired. Future investigations will determine whether such objects are confined to
certain districts, or whether they are not rather spread over
the whole face of the globe. For similar objects have already
been found in various parts of Asia, Africa, and America.

It must excite our astonishment that any uncivilized people
should be capable of producing such well-finished instruments of stone.   The arrow-heads figured above are so
admirably formed, that at the present day, with all the
advantage of our modern tools of metal, we could scarcely
equal, certainly could not surpass them ; even into the handles
of the knives very neatly executed ornaments are introduced ;
and yet it is supposed the use of metals was not understood.
We can easily see and understand how the arrow-head or axe
was first formed and afterwards polished; for indeed in several
instances the very whetstones have been found near such stone
implements ; we are also able to prove that the greater part
of the arrow-heads are formed of flints, which the makers knew
how to split out of large masses of that stone.   But the manner in which they contrived by means of a stone, so to split the
flint, and that too, into such long and slender pieces, is still a
mystery to us ; for from those uncivilized nations which still
make use of stone implements no satisfactory information has
yet been obtained as to the mode in which they manufacture
them.   Some have been of opinion that the aborigines endeavoured to prevent the splitting of the stone by boiling it, or
by keeping it under water while they fashioned it into the
desired form.   Others, on the contrary, have maintained, that
such stone implements could not possibly have been so well
formed by means of a stone, but must have been the work of
those who were possessed of the necessary metal.   Probably
the truth lies between these two opinions, namely, in the supposition, that in the earliest times, when the use of metals was
unknown, the stone implements were of the very simplest
make, but that at a later period, when some had attained to
the use of metals, they assumed a more perfect and handsome
form.   For it must be borne in mind that the use of instruments of stone unquestionably extended over a very long
period.

Lastly, we must not lose sight of this fact, that the weapons
and instruments of stone which are found in the north, in

Japan, in America, the South Sea Islands and elsewhere, have for the most part such an extraordinary resemblance to one another in point of form, that one might almost suppose the whole of them to have been the production of the same maker. The reason of this is very obvious, namely, that their form is that which first and most naturally suggests itself to the human mind.

These objects of stone are therefore not only of the highest interest to us, as monuments of the earliest inhabitants who traversed the extensive forests of Denmark, but also as examples of the earliest productions of human ingenuity which history has produced.

II. Antiquities of the Bronze-period.

If, without any reference to history, we should seek to determine which of the two metals, copper or iron, was first discovered and used for weapons and tools, we should very readily come to a conclusion in favour of that which is most easily recognised as a metal when in the earth. Now, we know that copper is found in the mines in a state of such comparative purity as to require very little smelting for the purpose of being brought into a state fit for use, while, on the other hand, iron in its rough state looks more like a stone than a metal, and, moreover, before it can be worked at all, must be subjected to a difficult process of smelting by means of a very powerful fire. If we look at the question only on this side, we are forced to conclude, that copper must have been found and employed before iron. And this is confirmed, not only by early historical notices, but also by recent investigations of ancient remains. In Asia, from whence the greater portion, probably all, the European races have migrated, numerous implements and weapons of copper have been discovered in a particular class of graves; nay, in some of the old and long abandoned mines in that country, workmen's tools have been discovered, made of copper, and of very remote antiquity. We see, moreover, how at a later period

attempts were made to harden copper, and to make it better
suited for cutting implements by a slight intermixture principally of tin.   Hence arose that mixed metal to which the
name of 'bronze' has been given, and which, according to the
oldest writers of Greece and Rome, was generally used in the
southern countries before iron.

That that was the case farther north, and that in Denmark there was once a time,—the so-called bronze-period,
—in which weapons and cutting instruments were made of
bronze, because the use of iron was either not known at all,
or very imperfectly, we learn with certainty from our antiquities.   We must not however by any means believe that the
bronze-period developed itself among the aborigines, gradually,
or step by step, out of the stone-period.   On the contrary,
instead of the simple and uniform implements and ornaments
of stone, bone, and amber, we meet suddenly with a number
and variety of splendid weapons, implements, and jewels of
bronze, and sometimes indeed with jewels of gold.   The transition is so abrupt, that from the antiquities we are enabled to
conclude, what in the following pages will be further developed, that the bronze-period must have commenced with the
irruption of a new race of people, possessing a higher degree
of cultivation than the early inhabitants.

As bronze tools and weapons spread over the land, the
ancient and inferior implements of stone and bone were, as a
natural consequence, superseded.   This change however was
by no means so rapid as to enable us to maintain with certainty, that from the beginning of the bronze-period, no stone
implements were used in Denmark.   The universal diffusion
of metals could only take place by degrees.   Since in Denmark itself, neither copper nor tin occurs, so that these metals,
being introduced from other countries, were, of necessity, expensive, the poorer classes continued for a long series of years
to make use of stone as their material; but it also appears
that the richer, at all events in the earlier periods, in addition
to their bronze implements, still used others of stone, parti-

cularly such as would have required a large quantity of metal for their formation. In tombs therefore which decidedly belong to the bronze-period, we occasionally meet with wedges and axes, knives and axes, but most frequently hammers, all of stone, which must have been used at a much later period. A great number of them are very carefully wrought, and also bear evident marks of having been bored through with round metal cylinders. But although implements of stone and bronze were at a certain period used together; yet it is an established fact that a period first prevailed during which stone alone was used for implements and weapons; and that, subsequently, a time arrived when the use of bronze appears to have been the all-prevailing custom.

Among the implements of bronze which are of most frequent occurrence are the Paalstabs [h] as they are called, which are from three to nine inches in length, of the shape of a chisel expanded towards the edge. They were fastened at the smaller end to a wooden handle[i]. They were probably used as a kind of axe or pickaxe, at all events similar tools of iron attached to wooden handles, are still used in

[h] This term Paalstab, was formerly applied in Scandinavia and Iceland, to a weapon used for battering the shields of the enemy, as is shewn by passages in the Sagas. Although not strictly applicable to the instrument in question, this designation is now so generally used by the antiquaries of Scandinavia and Germany, that it seems desirable with the view of securing a fixed terminology, that it should be introduced into the archæology of England.—T.

[i] In the curious paper on the Classification of Bronze Celts, contributed by Mr. Du Noyer to the Archæological Journal, we find the following example of one of the modes in which weapons of this form could be hafted.

It is taken from a specimen brought from Little Fish Bay in Africa, by Capt. Adams, R.N., and by that gentleman presented to Mr. Ball the Curator of the University Museum, Dublin.—T.

Iceland as crow-bars. There are many of these objects which have a regular cavity at the upper end for the handle. In a hill in Jutland a specimen was discovered which was fastened to the handle in the manner here figured.

The handle was not more than about eight inches in length, and was fastened beneath by three rings of leather. In several instances it has also been observed that the handle had been fastened by nails. From the inconsiderable length of the handle, it is scarcely probable that the Paalstab could have been intended for a weapon. It may occasionally have been used as such, but in general it was unquestionably employed merely for wood-work and for splitting stone.

Celts are instruments of another form. These are always hollowed out to receive a wooden handle, the ear[j], which is frequently introduced at the side, having probably served to fasten it to such handle by means of a thong.

[j] We are indebted to the same paper by Mr. Du Noyer for the following examples of celts.

The large ring on the ear of the

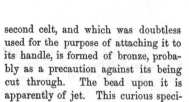

second celt, and which was doubtless used for the purpose of attaching it to its handle, is formed of bronze, probably as a precaution against its being cut through. The bead upon it is apparently of jet. This curious speci-men was found near Tadcaster in York-shire, and exhibited to the Society of Antiquaries by Mr. John Crosse, March 5, 1807. It is engraved in the Archæologia, vol. xvi. pl. 54.—T.

The axes of this period nearly resemble those of iron which are now in use, nor do the large knives offer any peculiarity, with the exception that some of them are crooked and formed exactly like a sickle. With iron knives of similar kind the corn is now cut in many places, particularly where the ground is so stony that large scythes are useless.

So important a change in the nature of the implements employed, as that from stone to metal, must naturally have exerted a very extensive influence on the mode of life, as well as on civilization in general. In the most ancient times the aborigines were compelled to follow hunting and fishing, and to construct their dwellings on the sea-coast, since with their imperfect implements they were scarcely able to pluck up the primeval forests by the roots and to engage in agriculture, a branch of industry to which the flat and fertile plains of Denmark are particularly adapted. As soon however as this difficulty was removed by the circumstance of the most cultivated and at the same time the most powerful part of the population becoming possessed of useful metallic implements, hunting and fishing were less followed, and instead of these occupations men began to till the earth. The inhabitants now no longer found sufficient space on the coasts, and having extirpated the forests in the interior of the country, partly by fire, partly by the axe, they spread themselves over the whole land, and at the same time laid the foundation for an agriculture, which up to the present day is one of the principal industrial resources of Denmark. From this time we must probably date the origin of villages; for the cultivation of the earth, and the peaceful employments connected with this pursuit, soon induced men to draw together, both for the purpose of affording mutual advice and assistance to each other, and also of combining to repel those hostile assaults which in such unquiet times were probably far from infrequent. But the inhabitants were by no means limited to the occupation of peaceful husbandry. Even in the stone-period the aborigines possessed boats or canoes, a consequence naturally arising from the intrusion of the sea into Denmark, but such rude vessels were at most employed merely for short voyages along the coast, or between the different parts of the land. At a later period, however, the introduction of a higher degree of civilization and the commerce with other countries thus occasioned, caused the inhabitants to be no longer satisfied with simple canoes hollowed out of stems of trees, but induced them to construct regular ships in which they could venture with confidence from the coast into the open sea. To sail across the ocean, and to wield the sword in sanguinary conflict, for the sake of winning glory and booty, formed from the earliest times the occupation and the delight of the inhabitants of the North. They were therefore evidently seamen as well as warriors. We may regard as memorials of their numerous sharp encounters with their enemies, the weapons which are exhumed in astonishing quantities from the barrows in which they were deposited, beside the ashes of the heroes who wielded them. Among such weapons the swords are particularly observable.

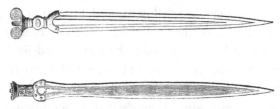

These occur so plentifully that hundreds have been collected, while many have perished in the course of time, and the earth still covers the greatest number of them. They are somewhat short, seldom more than two feet six inches in length, generally shorter and two-edged, so that the blade is thickest in the middle[k]. From this circumstance

---

[k] The following engraving represents a fine bronze sword of the kind termed by Sir S. Meyrick, Cleddyv, which measures 23¾ inches in length, and in the widest part of the blade 1¾ inch. Its weight is 23 oz.

It was found in Glamorganshire, and is now preserved in the Royal Institution at Swansea. A similar weapon of precisely the same length found at Fulbourn, Cambridgeshire, is in the possession of Sir S. Meyrick, who observes

it is probable that these swords were more used for stab-
bing than for cutting.   The hilts in some cases are of wood,
and have been fastened to the handle with nails; in
others they are of bronze melted and spread over a nucleus
of clay, the reason of which in all probability is that metal
was then very precious.   In some few specimens the
handles are covered with plates of gold, or wound round
with gold wire.   It is not superfluous to observe that these
handles are always very small, a fact which tends to prove
that the men who used these swords were but of moderate
stature and by no means so gigantic as many have represented
the ancient inhabitants of Denmark to have been.   The
scabbards for these swords, were of wood, covered both
externally and internally with leather, and also for the most
part guarded with metal at the end.   One of the peculiar characteristics of the bronze swords is that they were
never provided with guards at the handle, either in the form
of plates or points, and in this circumstance they differ from
all modern swords.   On the other hand, the daggers and
lance-heads of bronze were of a form similar to those of later
date, which are of iron.   The spear-heads were about twelve
inches in length[1], and were probably made for the insertion

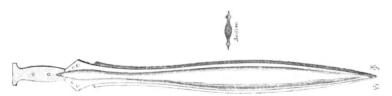

that the hilt was commonly formed of
horn, and hence the adage " he who
has the horn has the blade."—T.

[1] The following representations of
spear-heads are taken from the Archæological Journal, vol. ii. p. 187.

The first, which is six inches in
length, and has on either side of the

socket a lozenge-shaped projection, perforated in order to attach it to the shaft

by means of a strap, was discovered
in a bog, three miles south of Terman

of a wooden handle, at the end of which was introduced a point formed of metal.   Battle-axes of metal were also in use.

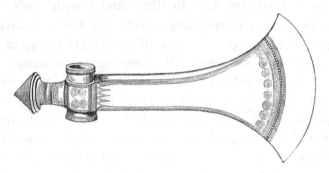

That which is here figured is of considerable size.   It is fifteen inches in length, and weighs not less than seven pounds. That battle-axes of this character formed of bronze were not unusual in the ages of antiquity is evident from the fact, that beside that already mentioned, two similar ones have been found in Scandinavia, one at Fühnen, the other at Schonen, of which however the latter alone is decorated with

Rock, on the road from Terman to Ballygawley, in the county of Tyrone.

The second, which was discovered at Peel in the Isle of Man, is five inches

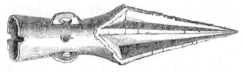

in length : and the third, which is of very singular fashion, the blade being flat and of greater breadth than usual, and terminating at the lower extremity,

in a shape more resembling the barbed head of an arrow, than the blade of a long handled weapon, was found in 1844, by some workmen who were

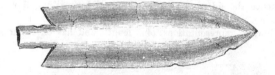

dredging in the bed of the Severn, about a mile and a half below Worcester.   It is now in the possession of Mr. Jabez Allies, F.S.A., weighs eight

ounces, and measures $10\frac{1}{4}$ inches in length, the breadth of the blade being $2\frac{3}{4}$ inches.—T.

spiral ornaments. It is moreover probable that the axes already mentioned among the implements, were employed on several occasions as weapons of warfare.

Nor did the Northmen at this period merely manufacture weapons of attack of so splendid and costly a character; their attention was equally directed to the means of protecting themselves from the swords of their enemies. Three large round shields have been discovered made entirely of bronze, the smallest of which, as figured below, is about nineteen, the two others about twenty-four inches in diameter.

These shields are formed of somewhat thin plates of bronze, the edge being turned over a thick wire of metal, to prevent the sword from penetrating too deeply. The handle is formed of a cross bar, placed at the reverse side of the centre boss, which is hollowed out for the purpose of admitting the hand[m]. In general, however, their shields were

[m] The following engravings represent a buckler of bronze, or metal, measuring in diameter 14 in. by 13, found
in 1836, in the pool of the Little Wit-

of a more simple kind, for instance of wood covered with leather, and sometimes also bordered with metal. There occur also round metal plates, with protruding points, which it is supposed must have covered the middle of such shields. They are in general very beautifully wrought, and adorned with the same kind of spiral ornaments as the battle-axe already mentioned.

Of helmets, one single relic alone has hitherto been discovered, namely the piece which covered the chin, together with two bars which went over the face. The chin-piece is partly gilded, that is, covered with a thin plate of gold, and on the whole of the exterior surface the most beautiful spiral ornaments are engraved. Though but a fragment, it is of

tenham or Day's Lock, upon the river Isis, about half a mile above the junction of that river with the Thame stream, and now in the British Museum.

It is ornamented with two series of

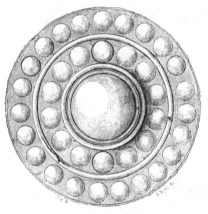 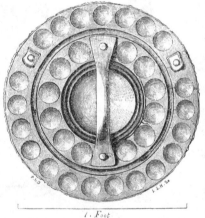

1. Foot

round bosses between raised concentric circles, having a large boss or umbo in the centre. All the bosses are punched in the metal except four, two of which form the rivets to the handle within, and two are the rivets to the metal extremities apparently of a strap, these four bosses being consequently move-

able. It is fully described in the Archæologia, vol. xxvii. p. 298.

For descriptions of two other specimens of bronze bucklers now at Somerset House, see pp. 16, 17 of Mr. Way's Catalogue of Antiquities, &c., in the possession of the Society of Antiquaries of London.—T.

course sufficient to shew that helmets were actually in use at this period.

Those remarkable objects designated Lures (*Luren*)[n], which were formed of molten bronze, must be regarded as war

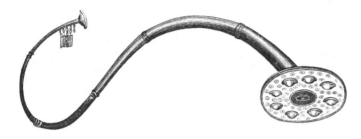

trumpets, with which the signal for attack was given. If they were stretched out to their full length they would in general be about six feet in length; when bent they are about three feet and a half long. In all probability the trumpet was borne by the player over the shoulder in such a manner that he held the mouth-piece with his right hand while with his left he grasped the broad disk; and therefore this disk being to be prominently shewn, was adorned with circular elevations and ring ornaments. In one single instance a long chain of metal was attached to the lure, being fastened to the mouth-piece and to the opposite end, an arrangement which must have proved eminently serviceable when the player wished to rest, or had to carry the instrument any great distance. Several of these lures are still in so good a state of preservation as to allow of being played upon, and their sound, which is something between the bugle and the trumpet, is not so dull as might be supposed.

Since their weapons and warlike implements were of such a kind, it cannot excite our wonder that these people possessed

[n] For an account of bronze trumpets found in Ireland, see Smith's Cork, vol. ii., and Gough's Camden, vol. iv. p. 231. The Dublin Penny Journal, vol. ii. pp. 27—30, contains a valuable Paper on the subject by Mr. Petrie, but in which no mention is made of a find of bronze trumpets near Dunmanway, in the county of Cork, which took place about twenty-five years ago, and of which two specimens are in the collection of Mr. Crofton Croker.—T.

a considerable quantity of trinkets, many of which were very
tasteful.   Large hair-pins, nearly a foot long, adorned with
knobs, and inlaid with gold and all kinds of ornaments;
combs, partly of bronze, partly of small pieces of bones
rivetted together ; rings for the hair of the most varied forms,

occasionally with broad expanded ends; and finally the so-
termed diadems, which beyond all doubt were fastened over
the forehead, all shew us that ornaments for the hair occupied
no mean place among the trinkets of that time.

They also wore round the neck rings, which were frequently hollow, doubtless for the purpose of being filled with
a soft substance, so as both to lessen their weight and pressure,
and at the same time to give them a more splendid appearance, and spare the metal.   Among the ornaments peculiar
to the age of bronze must be specified the winding spiral-
formed armlets, and which are generally upwards of twelve

inches in length, and therefore capable of covering almost the
whole of the arm.   Their flexibility secured this advantage,
that they could be expanded as the arm increased in circumference.   In some cases they might afford protection to the
arm against the blow of a sword.

But we know nothing with certainty as to the nature of the
costume which was most frequently worn in connection with
these ornaments.   That those who lived during the age of
bronze were not clad like the aborigines, chiefly in the skins
of animals, we may conclude from the degree of civilization to

which they had attained, and the rather because in the tombs of this period small pieces of woollen stuff are found, probably the remains of entire garments which have rotted away in the earth, and which are still woven in a very simple manner. Yet it is possible that these dresses were occasionally very neat and tasteful, for had they not been so the ornaments would not have produced suitable effect. At the same time it is by no means assumed that garments of skins or hides were never used; as from the nature of the climate if from no other cause, the inhabitants were compelled to wear furs, which of course were easily to be obtained in the country itself. The garments were either fastened together by double buttons, which resembled the studs or shirt buttons now in use, or by buckles or fibulæ, formed of two round plates of metal, connected by a small bar of iron, something resembling the shape of our spectacles, at the back part of which was placed a pin. Buckles or fibulæ also occur of different forms; they are sometimes made of a bent piece of metal, and are provided with a spiral-shaped spring, ending in a pointed pin, which enters an aperture fitted to receive it.

All these weapons and ornaments of bronze which we have here considered, when first discovered are usually covered with a greenish rust. On the rust being removed, the bronze is found to be so beautiful a metal that it might easily be mistaken for gold, did we not know that gold never rusts, however long it may be buried in the earth. Gold, however, as appears from our previous remarks on the inlaying of swords, helmets, and buttons, was by no means unknown at this time°. It was used both for bracelets and rings for the fingers, which are often formed of gold wire twisted in a

---

° The gold gorget from Dublin, described by Mr. Birch in his learned dissertation on the Torc of the Celts, in vol. iii. of the Archæological Journal, belongs to this period, as do also many of the gold ornaments found both in England and Ireland. A very interesting list of objects similar to the gorget in question, with the particulars of the several localities in which they

spiral shape, like the threads of the large bronze bracelets already mentioned. In several instances entire cups of gold have been found[p], of which the two last discovered, which were ploughed up at Boeslunde in the neighbourhood of Sla-

were found, will be seen in Mr. Birch's paper, to which we are indebted for the annexed engravings.—T.

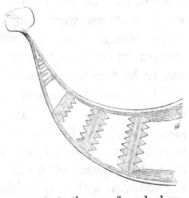

[p] The accompanying engraving represents a very curious object, also in fine gold, remarkable for the resemblance which it bears in its style of ornaments to the cup figured above, which was discovered two leagues from Poitiers, in March, 1844. It weighs about 11½ ounces, is 21 inches in

length, 5 inches in diameter at one end, and 1½ at the other. It is in the form of a divided cone, adorned with bands, charged alternately with four rows of pellets and ornaments, formed of four concentric circles, each band being separated by fillets. It has been cast entire at once, for there is no appearance of solder or rivets, and the ornaments have been struck from within outwards. It exhibits no appearance of any mode of suspension.

M. Lecointre Dupont, who forwarded the drawing to Mr. Roach Smith, writes, "To what people and epoch does this object belong, and what was its use, are questions to which I call your attention, and that

gelse, are seven inches in diameter at the mouth, and four inches in height. All the others which had been previously discovered are certainly considerably smaller. The use or object of these singular vessels is not easily explained, since nothing has yet been found with them capable of affording explanation on this point. Some persons have been of opinion that the larger were used as urns for ashes. For it was the custom in the bronze-period to burn the bodies of the dead on large funeral piles, after which the small portions of bone which remained, together with the ashes, were placed in the cinereal urns, as they were styled, and were deposited in barrows. These urns for ashes were usually formed of clay, and in the preparation of them considerable skill is displayed, but they also occur formed of metal, and as a rule are then distinguished by the neatness of their form and the tasteful character of their ornaments. In cases where the ashes and bones remaining from the consumed body were placed in the urn, they observed the custom of placing on the top of the bones and in the middle of the vessel various trifles of bronze, probably from some superstitious motive or other. Thus buttons, hair-pins[q], very small pincers, or as they are fre-

of the British Archæological Association. For my part I am tempted to assign this valuable relic to the Gauls, and I am pleased to find that M. Raoul Rochette, to whom it has been submitted, is of a similar opinion. The general notion is that it is a quiver, but in this I do not concur, believing rather that it may have been an orna-ment. I shall be happy to have your opinion on the subject, and to know if similar objects have been found in England."

No such object has, I believe, yet been discovered in England: but a similar one is preserved in the Museum at Munich.—T.

[q] The bronze pin here figured, and

which is remarkable for having its head hollowed like a cup, and bearing in this respect a striking resemblance to the ends of the golden ornaments often found in Ireland, was discovered on an island in a lake near Carrickmacross, in the autumn of 1844. See Archæological Journal, vol. iii. p. 49.—T.

quently termed, pinzetten, of the form here figured, together with needles, which were qua-drangular at one end, and at the other pointed, and stuck like awls in handles of wood or

bronze ; and lastly knives, which were somewhat small, and with bent handles, and occasionally had some very beautifully engraved ornaments on one side.

These last-mentioned objects appear to have been partly used in sewing, and are usually found together[r].

In considering the various antiquities of the bronze-period, our attention cannot but be struck by the manner in which they are wrought, and the very considerable degree of skill displayed in their construction. The greater part of the objects are cast, but the casting is neither rude nor common. In this point of view a very remarkable battle-axe of bronze re-quires particular mention. It is sixteen inches in length, and is ten inches broad at the edge. At the end of the neck there is a very handsome knob, and one of similar kind surmounts the hole made to the handle, and in which the remains of the wooden shaft still exist. Along the broad sides are circular cavities, with a raised knob in the middle of them, into part of

[r] The bronze instrument here repre-sented, which appears to be a kind of falx or pruning hook, is now deposited in the British Museum. It measures four inches from the extremity of the blade to the back of the socket, into which the handle was inserted and fixed by a rivet. It was found at the depth of six feet, in a bog, in the vicinity of the mountain range two miles east from Ballygawley, in the county of Tyrone. A woodcut repre-senting "one of the ancient bronze reaping-hooks, so frequently found in Ireland, and which from its material

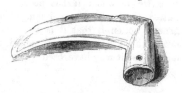

must be of the most remote antiquity," which bears a general resemblance to the foregoing object, is given in the Dublin Penny Journal, vol. i. p. 108, in illustration of Mr. John O'Dona-van's remarks on the Antiquity of Corn in Ireland.—T.

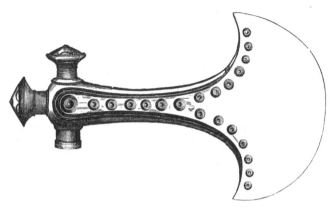

which a thin plating of gold has been inlaid. The axe is also embellished with ornaments imitating flame. This splendid specimen is composed of a very small portion of metal, cast upon a nucleus or filling of clay, which extends as far as the edge, so that the axe in point of fact consists merely of clay, coated with a thin plating of metal. Hence it is probable that it was never used as a weapon, but rather perhaps as an emblem of command, a sort of general's baton, or something of a similar nature.

Not less remarkable than this skill in casting, is the height to which the art of working in gold had been attained at so early a period. This circumstance will be most clearly evinced by the fact that the beautiful gold cup figured above (p. 36,) like the others of the same kind has been hammered from a massive piece of gold. Among many other very elegant bronze objects, a portion of a small and very thinly cast vessel has been preserved, in which traces of inlaid work are perceptible. On the lower side are ornaments in the form of rays of light, which are deeply engraved, and are filled up with a black substance, which is now in a partially dissolved state. The ornaments on the whole deserve particular attention, not only on account of the care and skill with which they are for the most part executed, but in particular because they are of a peculiar kind, such as never occur in so decided a form either before or after this period. We possess therefore in these objects a tolerably certain means of determining how far any articles of bronze thus discovered may be regarded as belonging to the bronze-period or not; and by enquiring in what countries similar antiquarian ornaments exist, we shall doubtless in time arrive at a better knowledge of the relations which the then existing nations bore to each other than we now possess. The most characteristic ornaments of the bronze period, and at the same time those most frequently used, but which, as might be expected, occur with more or less of variation, may be arranged in four classes. Spiral ornaments

Spiral Ornament.

Double Spiral.

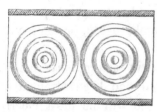

Ring Ornament.

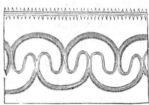

Wave Ornament.

are the most peculiar, and also the most ancient. The ring ornaments occur particularly on objects of larger size, for instance on the lures or trumpets, shields, and the like, and appear to be more modern[s]; while the wave ornaments may be regarded as the most modern, and as forming the transition to those ornaments which became general in the iron-period.

The question will here very naturally arise, were these bronzes wrought in Denmark itself, or were they brought in a finished state from other countries. The answer to this question is not without importance to our history. For if we

[s] Similar designs, namely designs consisting of concentric rings, are found on the gold ornaments discovered in Ireland.—T.

can assume that these objects are actually native productions, we here have a decided proof that its inhabitants in the bronze-period were in possession of a certain degree of civilization. A rude people, who led a savage and warlike life, without possessing either a knowledge or a love of the arts of peace, could scarcely have possessed either mind or energy to produce works which often display both taste and skill of a striking kind.

That our bronze antiquities were brought by the Romans, who by their conquests in Gaul and Britain during the first centuries after the birth of Christ occasioned a complete revolution in the civilization of the north-west of Europe, is altogether incredible. It is true that there occur in Italy a number of bronze implements and weapons which are somewhat similar to our own, as for instance paalstabs, celts and spear-heads, but as these bronzes want the peculiar ornaments above described, they prove nothing more than that certain implements and weapons had the same form among different nations. It is besides a settled point that the Romans when they made war in Gaul and in Britain, had long been in possession of iron, and made use of weapons which were of a totally different form from the bronze weapons found in Denmark. Nor in all probability have these bronzes reached us from Greece, although both with regard to their form and ornaments, particularly the spiral ornaments, a greater similarity appears to exist between those which occur in the North, and those found in the most ancient tombs of Greece. For independently of the fact that the latter have hitherto occurred but seldom, so that our knowledge of them is extremely imperfect, they belong to so very remote a period, 1000 or 1400 years before the birth of Christ, that we can by no means be justified in supposing that any active intercourse then existed between countries so remote from each other. If on the other hand we reflect that the bronzes here described with their peculiar spiral ornaments occur within certain limits of the North, it certainly

G

may not be altogether improbable that we must look for
their manufacture at home, or within such limits.   Hitherto
they have been met with in the greatest number in Denmark and the neighbouring province of Mecklenburg, but
they have about the same northerly limit as the stone
objects, while they occur but singly in the provinces immediately beyond the ancient Danish land of Schonen, and
scarcely at all in the north of Sweden, or in Norway.   In
England, Ireland, France, the south and east districts of the
north of Germany, as well as in Hungary, cutting instruments and other antiquities of bronze are met with, but in
none of the countries named, as far as is known, do they
completely accord with those of Denmark and Mecklenburg;
that is, they are never adorned with spiral ornaments like
those of Denmark and its vicinity.   The native character of
these objects is farther evidenced by the fact that in Mecklenburg, a number of bronzes have been found accompanied by
the moulds in which they were cast[t], together with pieces of

[t] The following cuts exhibit speci-   British Islands; the first, 1 and 2, taken
mens of celt-moulds discovered in the   from the Archæological Journal, vol. iii.

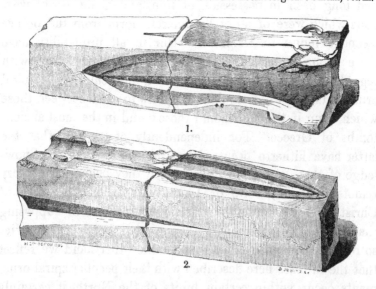

1.

2.

unwrought metal; and that in Denmark collections of broken weapons, tools, and ornaments intended for smelting have

p. 257, represent the moiety of a set of moulds for casting spear-heads and celts of bronze formed of hone-stone, which was found between Bodwrdin and Tre Ddafydd, in the western part of the Isle of Anglesea. It measures, in length, nine inches and a quarter : each side measures, at one extremity two inches, and at the other one inch and a half. It is obvious that with a second precisely similar piece of stone, four complete moulds for casting ob-

jects of various forms would be obtained, comprising a celt of simple form with a loop on the side for the purpose of attaching it to the haft, spear-heads of two sizes, with lateral loops for a like purpose, and a sharp pointed spike four inches and a half in length, probably intended to be affixed to a javelin, or some missile weapon. Figures 3 and 4, first engraved for Mr. Du Noyer's interesting papers on Celts and Celt Moulds, in the fourth

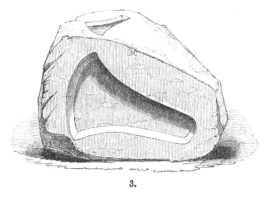

3.

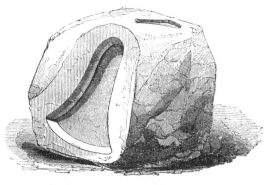

4.

volume of that Journal, exhibit a celt-mould of which the original is now at Belfast. The stone is polygonal in form, and exhibits upon four of its

surfaces indented moulds for celts of the normal type, the two largest (fig. 3.) measure 6 inches in length, by 4¼ at the blade, and (fig 4.) 5 inches in

been found: and that among other objects a thin bronze vessel
has been discovered which is filled inside with the thick hard
mass of clay over which it was cast and which could scarcely
have been brought from a foreign country.   Still less would
any one have brought hither the casting as it is technically
styled, that is, the small portion of metal which in casting
runs into the aperture and is subsequently removed in finish-
ing the object.   But since similar pieces are found here in
connection with antiquities appertaining to the bronze-period,
the casting and the other work must in all probability have
been executed on the spot; from which circumstance it may
be observed that the most ancient forms and ornaments have
been introduced with the knowledge of metals, rather than
conceived originally in the North.   In like manner the bronze
and the gold, which are nowhere found in the country, are of
foreign introduction.   These metals might easily have been
introduced, in the rude state, either from Russia, from the
Ural mountains, or from England, where, as is well known,
tin and copper, the constituents of bronze, occur in considerable quantities, and where gold may have been found in

length, by 3 and 3¾ at the blade.   But
these celt-moulds were sometimes made
of bronze ; and the accompanying engravings represent one of this material now preserved in the British Museum.—T.

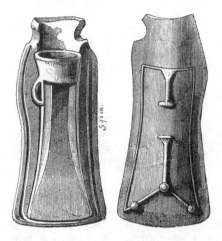

ancient times: while we may account for its presence here either by supposing that the transit took place direct by sea, or that the metal was first transmitted to countries nearer England, and thence by barter was brought to the North. This fact, at least, is evident, that almost all bronzes which are referable to that primeval time, when iron was not generally known or employed, are formed of a peculiar mixture of metals, which is constantly the same in all the countries in which they are found. It contains for instance about nine tenths of copper and one tenth of tin, while the more modern bronze which, subsequently to the knowledge of iron, was used for ornaments, vessels, and the like, was usually formed of equal quantities of copper and zinc. Hence it is highly probable that the ancient bronze formed of copper and tin, was diffused from one spot over the whole of Europe; which spot may be supposed to be England, because, not to mention the quantity of copper which that country produces, its rich tin mines have been known from the earliest historic periods to the nations of the south, while in the other parts of Europe there occur only very few and doubtful remains of other and far less important tin mines, which we are justified in believing to have been worked at that time. It must however be observed, that according to Cæsar the Britons in his time used imported bronze, (*ære utuntur importato.*)

Hitherto no inscriptions or traces of characters have been discovered in the antiquities of the bronze-period, although judging from their skill in working metals, it would not be unreasonable to suppose that the people, at all events, towards the close of that period, may have understood the art of writing.

III. ANTIQUITIES OF THE IRON-PERIOD.

As our native land evinced a peculiar developement in the bronze-period, so during that of iron it yielded to that more modern civilization which, by degrees, diffused itself over

Europe. Not only had civilization at length attained to such
a point that all cutting instruments were made of iron, but at
the same time a new taste had established itself in the North.
The difference between the bronze-period and that of iron,
consists not only in the circumstance that in the iron-period
people continued to make use of iron for those objects which
they had previously formed of bronze, (for they still continued
to use this latter metal for trinkets, vessels, &c.,) but it is
displayed essentially by the fact, that the character of all. the
works in the iron-period both with reference to their material but more particularly to their forms, their ornaments and
their workmanship in general, is completely changed. It
is however not possible to indicate with clearness or precision, any gradual transition from the ancient to the modern
taste.

The period in which this alteration may have taken place
is difficult to determine; since the ancient Sagas and traditions do not make any mention of the inhabitants of this
country being compelled for want of iron to use implements
and weapons of bronze. Meanwhile it will appear from enquiries which we shall pursue in future pages, that the bronze
period was in all probability supplanted at a comparatively
modern date, since all the objects in the succeeding age,
plainly exhibit the influence of a more modern civilization;
and at all events the close of paganism is clearly reflected in
this iron-period. In treating of this epoch we feel more
confidence than in the period either of stone or of bronze,
because we possess a tolerable number of written memorials
on which we may rely, when explaining many of the antiquities belonging to it.

Christianity first began to be generally diffused in the
North about 900 years ago. Up to that time, the people of
the North were mere heathens, who acknowledged a religion
which chiefly excited them to conflicts and to deeds of arms.
They believed that those heroes alone who fell in the field,
would go to Odin the god of the brave, or enter into Val-

halla, the abode of the blessed. Here they should pass their time in joy and delight. During the day it was said the fallen giants contended in a forest before Valhalla, until they fell beneath each other's blows, but towards evening they came to life again and rode back to Valhalla. Wearied with the fight, they refreshed themselves here by a splendid banquet; and in common with the gods feasted on the swine Särimner, whose flesh constantly renews itself, nor did they forget to drink plentifully of the choicest beer and mead.

As valour was regarded as the highest virtue, so cowardice was stamped as the basest of crimes. From his earliest youth the native of the North sought for warlike fame. While a mere stripling the Northman practised the use of the sword, which when he had grown to manhood he never allowed to rust in its scabbard. If there were no troubles at home to afford him the opportunity of displaying his courage, he adopted the predatory life of a Viking, and eagerly undertook warlike expeditions, or made descents upon foreign countries, for the purpose of winning both glory and booty. In the winter, he sate at home in his hall surrounded by his retainers; but in the spring he again took to the sea, and frequently encountered other Vikings[u], from the North. Joining their forces they visited with their terrors not only the countries of the Baltic, but also England and France, whose coasts were scarcely ever free from their plundering visitations; and even countries lying farther to the south, as Italy and Spain:

[u] The English reader desirous of knowing the nature of the Vikings, is referred to Laing's Introduction to his translation of the Heimskringla, (i. p. 45,) who says in a note, "The *Viking* is a word not connected with the word *Konge*, or king. Vikings are merely pirates, alternately peasants and pirates, deriving the name of Viking from the *viks*, wicks or inlets, on the coasts in which they harboured with their long ships or rowing galleys. Every sea-king was a Viking; but every Viking was not a sea-king."

Mohnike in his German translation of the Heimskringla, speaks very highly of the Swedish work of Strinholm, on the subject of the Vikings, and the early history of Scandinavia, published at Stockholm in 1834, under the title *Skandinavien under Hedna-Aldern*, a German translation of which by Frisch, appeared at Hamburgh in 1839.—T.

and wherever they committed their ravages and devastation they left sanguinary traces of their formidable swords.

The peculiar life of the Viking, in accordance with which single warriors (Vikings) undertook each on his own account continual expeditions to foreign countries, appears to have had its home chiefly in Norway and in Sweden; a fact which may be readily accounted for, since the mountainous and woody character of these countries, which are but little calculated for agriculture, compelled the inhabitants of them to seek for subsistence in lands better provided than their own. On the other hand in a country so flat, and in some parts, so fertile as Denmark, where agriculture had early taken root, a considerable number of its inhabitants were probably engaged in the cultivation of the fields; from which circumstance we may the more easily explain the fact, which is related of the Danes, that in general they did not so often undertake these predatory expeditions singly, as in larger bodies, which were commanded by kings or chiefs of royal descent. Numbers of Danish warriors, who yielded neither in bravery nor cruelty to the other Northmen, made extensive conquests among other nations, towards the conclusion of the eighth and during the whole of the ninth century; when all the small Danish kingdoms were united under one ruler, Gorm the ancient. From this period these expeditions ceased for a time, while Christianity diffused itself by degrees over the country, but the ancient rude warrior spirit, and the lust of conquest which inspired the nation, were not subdued without considerable resistance. The first Christian king, Harald Blaatand, (about 990,) was slain in a tumult of the heathens, and his son Svend Tveskiäg, who destroyed the churches, and slew or drove out the Christians, again undertook expeditions to England, which he at length conquered, after having, according to the pagan custom, fearfully wasted it by fire and sword. His successor Knut the Great it was who first established Christianity, and with it more gentle manners in Denmark. To so warlike a people as the heathenish Danes, and in so troubled a time, when no man could feel safe from the attacks of strangers, and all were consequently obliged to be constantly prepared for conflict, good weapons were naturally of extraordinary importance. Skilful armourers were then in great request, and although in other cases the Danish warrior would have thought it unbecoming and dangerous to disturb the peace of the dead, he did not scruple to break open a barrow, or a grave, if by such means he could obtain the renowned weapon which had been deposited beside the hero who had wielded it.

The iron swords of this period were somewhat larger than those of bronze, but more rarely two edged[x].

At the end of the handle, which was covered with wood, leather, bone, or stag's horn, which however is now consumed, a tolerably large knob or boss was introduced, with the view of forming a counterpoise to the blade. The introduction of a guard also indicates a nearer approach to the more regular form of swords. The handle, or to speak more correctly, the knob and the guard, among the rich, were surrounded with chains of gold, or covered with plates of gold and silver; and

---

[x] The reader cannot but be struck with the obvious resemblance between the decorations on the handle of the sword figured above, and the interlaced ornaments observable in MSS., and other productions of the Anglo-Saxons, and of which the accompanying engravings, which exhibit por-

tions of two crosses of the Anglo-Saxon period, preserved in the Museum of the Literary and Philosophical Institution of Bath, furnish very characteristic examples.—T.

swords with handles entirely of silver have also been discovered. In general the handles of the iron swords are
longer than those of the bronze, but still without having,
on this account, a striking or unusual size. The sheaths,
which were chiefly made of wood, and covered with leather,
in addition to the buckle and the other metallic ornaments, were also adorned at the
end nearest the handle with a massive, oblong, flat gold ring of considerable value.

This latter object was often beautifully adorned with winding patterns; and in one instance a small clasp was introduced at the upper side, probably for the purpose of fastening
the thong with which they bound the handle, to prevent the
sword from being drawn from its scabbard.

The high estimation in which our ancestors held their
swords, will appear from the circumstance that the heroes
usually gave names to them, which afterwards lived in the
songs of the Scalds. Thus, according to tradition, " Skrep"
was the name of the sword which Vermund the Wise gave
to his son Uffe, when he went forth to fight against the
haughty Saxons, and there was no other sword which would
have been proportioned to his strength; Rolf Krage's sword
was named " Skofnung[y]."

Among the other weapons of attack beside swords, were
battle axes, somewhat broad, but very simple in form.
Neither the lance nor the spear was distinguished by any
particular formation. Javelins also appear to have been
much used, as several different kinds of them are mentioned
in the Sagas[z]. In this class it has been supposed that we are

[y] Tycho Rothe wrote a Dissertation
"De Gladiis veterum in primis Dano-
rum," which is printed in the first
volume of Oelrich's Suecia et Dania
litterata. For the history of Balmung,
Mimung, and other swords of the great
heroes of Teutonic Romance, the
reader is referred to 'Die Deutsche Hel-
densage' of William Grimm.—T.

[z] The antiquary who may be desirous of comparing the weapons used
by the early inhabitants of the north
of Europe, with those which were
adopted by the natives of the British
Islands, may consult Bircherode's *Pa-
læstra Antiquaria*, 8vo. Hafn. 1688;
P. II. Jahn's *Norden's Krigsvafen i
Mittelalerén*, 8vo. Copenhagen, 1825;

to include the spears with hooks, not unfrequently found in the graves, and which were fitted for the insertion of a wooden handle. The handle itself was furnished with a thong, to give increased force to the throw; and appears to have been partially split at the end, and to have been furnished with feathers. The little arrows which were used for shooting birds, were of course by no means so large as the javelins. They were not merely three and four edged, but usually flat, and occasionally furnished with barbed hooks. Among the most usual weapons of defence, the ancient Sagas mention helmets, coats of mail, armour, and shields. The fact that of the three first-named objects scarcely any relics at all have reached us, is by no means difficult to explain. The helmets, which were furnished with crests, usually in the shape of animals[a], were probably in most cases only the skins of the heads of animals, drawn over a frame-work of wood or leather, as the coat of mail was usually of strong quilted linen, or thick woven cloth. Lastly, the armour which covered the breast was formed, it is true, of metal, either in iron rings attached to each other, or of plates fastened on each other like scales, but it certainly was only a few individuals who had the means and opportunity of obtaining such expensive objects. The shields, on the other hand, were in general use; they had commonly the same form as the shields of the bronze-

and lastly C. C. Rafn's *Krigsvafenets Forsatning under Knud den Store*, 8vo. Copenhagen, 1818.—T.

[a] The animal generally represented was the boar, and it is to this custom that reference is made in Beowulf when the poet speaks of the hog of gold, the boar hard as iron.

 Swyn eal-gylden
 Eofer iren-heard,—ll. 2217, 18, ed.
 Kemble.

Nor are allusions to this remarkable custom of wearing the figure of a boar, —not in honour of that animal, but of Freya to whom it was sacred,—con-

fined to Beowulf. They are to be found in the Edda and in the Sagas, while Tacitus, in his *De Mor. Germ.* distinctly refers to the same usage and its religious intention; when speaking of the Aestii, he says, " Matrem Deum venerantur Aestii; insigne superstitionis formas aprorum gestant. Id pro armis omnique tutelâ securum Deæ cultorem etiam inter hostes præstat." See further Ettmuller's Beowulf, (Zurich, 1840,) p. 50. In this practice it is obvious that we may recognise the origin of the more modern crests.—T.

period[b], though they were not wholly composed of metal, but consisted of a frame of wood, covered with leather, in the midst of which was an iron boss, which received and protected the hand.

[b] The annexed cut represents the boss of a shield of the usual Saxon form, which with the accompanying horse's bit, buckle, and fragment of iron, (consisting of one large and two smaller rings,) were found in a barrow in Bourne Park, near Canterbury, opened by Lord Albert Conyngham, on the occasion of the British Archæologists visiting Canterbury.

The next engraving is from the boss

of a shield discovered in a tumulus on Breach Downs, near Canterbury, by the same nobleman in the month of September, 1841; the opening and examination of which are very fully described by his lordship in the Archæologia, vol. xxx. pp. 47—56.

While the following cuts from the

Journal of the Archæological Association, vol. ii. p. 53, represent two bosses of very characteristic forms, differing however very considerably from those generally found in Kent and in the Isle of Wight, and which were discovered in 1844-5, in a field called Tanner's field, which from time immemorial has remained unbroken, and lies on the outskirts of Fairford, in Gloucestershire. T.

They were almost always painted, and inlaid with gold, or ornamented with figures in relief; occasionally symbols were introduced into the shield, which gave rise to the introduction of armorial bearings, as every succeeding race preserved its own particular symbol.

A nearer examination of the weapons here mentioned would suffice to shew that the purity in the form and workmanship, which we so much admired in the bronze-period, had been supplanted, and had given place to a totally different taste. We no longer find anything corresponding to the splendid swords, battle-axes, bosses of shields, and lures. But this difference becomes more plain and obvious when we place before our eyes the trinkets and ornaments of the iron-period.

As a characteristic ornament of this period, we must point out the oval *shell*-shaped breast-clasps, as they are termed, of brass. They consist chiefly of a convex plate of metal which is usually gilded, to which another metal plate is attached, having open-work and loop ornaments, so that the gilding of the lower plate shewed through. On the reverse

 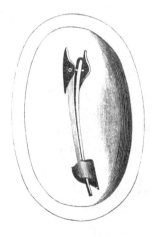

the iron pin of the brooch is placed. Probably they may have served as female ornaments; and they are found usually in pairs, whence we may conclude that they were worn one

on each breast. That they are positively to be referred
to the last period of paganism, we know with complete certainty, because they are frequently found
in graves in Ireland[c], which country was
first peopled by pagan Norwegians, at
the close of the ninth century. In connection with these oval ornaments, some
other clasps, called the trefoil-shaped
clasps, were occasionally deposited.

On the obverse they are embellished with the loop ornaments; on the reverse an iron pin is introduced, which is fastened in a ring. It is therefore evident that these were also
clasps. Although there are several different ornaments of the
same kind, we will pass over them as of minor importance,
and call attention to the numerous gold ornaments of the
same period. In the bronze-period most of the ornaments
were of the common metals, occasionally covered with thin

[c] The following engravings from the
Journal of the Archæological Association, vol. ii. p. 331, represent two
similar objects found at Pier-o-wall in
Orkney, in April, 1839. They are of
bronze or copper, and to the projecting
points presented on the exterior convex
surface, jewels, stones, or glass were no
doubt affixed. The bow-like bar in the
concavity of No. 3, is of iron. In the

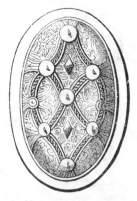

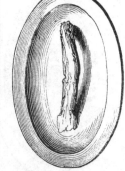

Vetusta Monumenta (vol. ii. pl. 20.
figs. ix. and x.) a similar ornament is
engraved, which was found together
with a brass pin and a brass needle,
one on each side of a skeleton, in the

Isle of Sangay, between the Isles of
Uist and Harris, to the west of Scotland: and there is a similar object in
the British Museum.—T.

gold plates, and much more rarely of massive gold; now the very reverse is the case. At the same time we do not find the gold altogether unalloyed. It was used with a portion of silver, fused with it, by which a metal has been produced to which the name of electrum has been given. Objects of pure silver alone, which, it is known, have never been discovered in barrows together with remains from the bronze-period, also occur in this period, although they are by no means so general in Denmark as articles of gold.

The superior style of these trinkets, as they are occasionally found, will appear from the circumstance that our forefathers also possessed ornaments for the head, which were of massive gold. That which is here figured was found some years ago at Starup, in the neighbourhood of Haderslev,

and is particularly remarkable, because on the reverse of the broad plate, which probably adorned the forehead, is seen the word ᚠᚢᚦᚱᚲ (lvþro), which probably denoted the name of its possessor. In case the name of a man was here expressed, which is not improbable, the inscription would tend to confirm the former supposition, that it was by no means women only, but doubtless men also, who were adorned with such ornaments. It will be impossible at the present day to determine whether rings were worn in ancient times exclusively by men or women, for which reason we will treat of these ornaments together.

Still larger and more costly than the ornaments for the head just described, are the rings which in all probability were worn round the neck[d]. They are composed of two

---

[d] We are indebted to Mr. Birch's elaborate paper on the Torc of the Celts, in the third vol. of the Archæological Journal, for the accompanying figure of a solid torc, now in the collection of the British Museum. The body is plain but thin, the bulbs oblong, slightly concave, and decorated at the side with an engrailing. This has been anciently twisted into a knot, probably in order to fit a younger or female wearer, or perhaps it has been

separate rings, each of which
forms about three fourths of
a circle, and which are held
together by two small clasps.
To attach these ornaments
round the neck, it was necessary to separate the rings,
and to unite the ends again
by means of these clasps.
They thus presented the
same appearance as if the
wearer had had two very

valuable gold rings round his neck, which appeared more
splendid than they actually were, because the more massive
portion of each ring was turned outwards on the breast.
These rings were also adorned with wrought
plates of gold, in which pieces of coloured
glass were occasionally inlaid, but they were
more frequently hung round with gold
bracteates, as they were termed. These were
formed of very thin plates, one side of which
is, in some cases, stamped with an imitation
of the coins of foreign countries.

These bracteates[e] are however in general of so peculiar a

intended for an armilla, since two more
of these were found with it.—T.

  [e] In the Archæologia, vol. xxxii. pp.

64, et seq., will be found a paper by
Sir Henry Ellis, on the subject of a
jewel or ornament composed of an
ancient cast from a gold coin of the
Emperor Mauricius, set into gold of
rough workmanship, with a ring or
loop at the top to suspend it by, and bits
of red glass or stone let in, in a double
row on that side which bears the
obverse of the coin, forming a border
to it, and to which a rich appearance
is given by bits of stamped gold being
placed under each. This curious relic,
obviously of the class alluded to in the
text, was found upon the beach of the
Norfolk coast, between Bacton and

character, that it is either wholly impossible, or at all events
extremely difficult, to ascertain the original coins after which
they are wrought. The Runic inscriptions which are frequently
introduced in the margin, have afforded but little explanation, since it has not as yet been possible to interpret the
many peculiar Runic characters of which the inscriptions
consist.   In general however we may assume with confidence
that the coins of Eastern Rome and Arabia have furnished
the original of these imitations.   Roman and Oriental coins
themselves were also used for ornaments of this kind, when
furnished with a border and a loop.   Gold bracteates have
been found of various sizes, from half an inch to six inches
in diameter.   In general they occur either in connection
with several similar ones, so that they must originally have
formed whole necklaces, or they are found with different kinds
of beads.

As such beads formed a very favourite ornament in ancient
times, and also deserve a peculiar degree of attention, on
account of their nature and construction, we shall here introduce a more detailed account of them. The most simple are
of amber and burnt clay, the others of rock crystal, cornelian,
gold, silver, or some other metal; the latter being usually
very thin, and filled within with clay; they were also constructed of glass, and finally of mosaic, as it was termed.
At the period which we are considering glass could scarcely
have been manufactured in the North.   It must have been

Mundesley, in January, 1846, and was
then in the possession of Miss Gurney,
but has since been presented by her to
the British Museum, which previously
possessed three similar specimens, also
described by Sir H. Ellis.

In the Journal of the Archæological
Association, vol. ii. p. 314, will be found
a description and engraving of a very
curious bracteate fibula, obtained from
a barrow in the parish of Ottley, Norfolk, about twelve years ago. It is of
bronze patinated; and from the resemblance which the figure upon it
bears to that upon the seal of Richard
Constable of Chester, in the time of
Stephen, or that upon the coins ascribed to Robert, earl of Gloucester,
the illegitimate son of Henry I., Mr.
Fairholt is inclined to conclude that it
is a work of the same period.

Would not the fact of coins being
thus used as ornaments, and not as
money, seem to indicate their rarity at
the period when they were so employed?—T.

brought from other countries, and was therefore unquestionably of considerable rarity; on which account beads of
common white or green glass were also used. For the purpose of giving these glass beads a resemblance to gold, they
were occasionally covered with a thin plating of that metal,
over which again was poured a slight layer of glass. Such
beads formed the transition between beads of gold and of
mosaic. Those of mosaic consist either of clay, in which
pieces of coloured glass and bits of enamel are inlaid, or,
(which is however much more rarely the case,) of glass
globules which, with admirable skill, are first covered with
plates of gold, and pieces of glass of the most varied colours,
together with bits of enamel, and then again are overlaid with
a coating of glass, through which may be seen the gold and
the variegated colours[f]. Of such beads, which are equally
distinguished for beauty and skilful workmanship, there have
been found in Denmark four of such a size that some persons
have considered them to be knobs for the handles of swords;
we must however observe, that it has not yet been decided
whether they really belong to pagan times.

[f] The bead here represented
(from Arch. Journal, vol. iii. p. 354)
is in the possession of Mr. Orlando
Jewitt, of Headington, Oxford, and,
it is believed, was found in that
neighbourhood. It appears almost
black, but when held to the light is
found to be a beautifully clear deep
green glass. The surface of it is
richly varied with splashes of white
enamel mixed with blue, radiating
from the centre and slightly con-
torted, particularly on the under
side. The enamel penetrates some
distance into the surface of the glass,
and appears to have been thrown on to
the mass while in a soft state; it was
then probably slightly twisted, and its
globular form flattened down between
two plain surfaces. It is not perforated, and there is only a slight de-

pression in the centre. Another bead
of similar character, found near Adder-
bury, in the same county, and now
deposited in the Ashmolean Museum,
is engraved in Beesley's History of
Banbury.—T.

Among all the ornaments of pagan antiquity, none are more frequently mentioned in the ancient Sagas than the armlets. We often read of kings and chieftains presenting armlets to bards who had sung their heroic deeds, as well as to others whom they wished, for some reason or other, to honour and reward. Thus King Rolf presented the hero Viggo with two gold armlets, because he had bestowed on the king the name of Krake. The gold armlets which are now exhumed are sometimes shaped like bands or ties, sometimes they are formed of two gold bars, or of a single weighty bar, the ends of which are thicker than the other parts of the ring, and do not shut close; and again with the outward side beaten out broad, and embellished with ornaments[g]. Occasionally a long gold bar is twisted in a spiral  form several times round the arm. The rings are usually solid, and even at the present day are of considerable value. This is also the case to a certain degree with regard to the finger-rings. The largest of them are very broad in front[h]; others, found less frequently, are adorned with a border, consisting of pieces of glass; all of these are usually of simple form, in many cases indeed they are such as might be used at the present day.

The silver rings which furnished an ornament for the head or neck as well as the arms, have not been mentioned hitherto, partly because they were very frequently used as money in commercial transactions, and partly because they differ

[g] Sir Philip de Malpas Grey Egerton, Bart., exhibited to the Society of Antiquaries two gold bracelets of this form which were found in 1831 in digging the foundation of a cottage near Egerton Hall, Cheshire. See Archæologia, vol. xxvii. p. 401, where one of them is engraved.—T.

[h] A very curious and interesting gold Saxon ring, inscribed NOMEN EHLÆA FIDES IN XPO, found in a meadow at Bosington, near Stockbridge, Hants, by a labourer who saw it glittering among the peat, and which is now in the possession of the Rev. A. B. Hutchings, of Appleshaw, Hants, is engraved in the Journal of the Arch. Association, vol. i. p. 341.—T.

in form and workmanship from similar articles in gold.
Most commonly they were
either composed of several
thin plates twisted to-
gether[i], or, like the armlet
here figured, were con-
structed of a single bar
beaten flat[k], the outer side

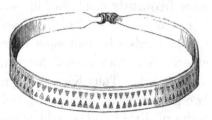

i The accompanying engraving, derived from Mr. Birch's paper in the
Arch. Journal, to which such frequent

allusion has already been made, represents a Saxon torc of silver, found at
Halton Moor with coins of Canute,

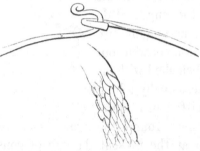

which is remarkable for having the
body composed of many small chains,

and having the upper part ornamented
with triangular stamped ornaments

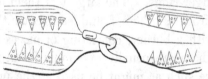

with pellets, a mode of ornamentation
very commonly found on the antiquities discovered both in Scandinavia
and in this country.—T.

k A number of similar armlets were
found with Anglo-Saxon coins, pieces
of the second race of French kings, and
Cufic coins, at Cuerdale, near Preston,
in 1840, and the following (see next
page) is one of many figured in Mr.
Hawkins's interesting paper on the
subject, in the 4th vol. of the Arch.
Journal. While on this subject I cannot resist quoting from the same volume the following extract from M.
Worsaae's remarks on those antiquities.

" Hildebrand, in describing the Cufic
or oriental coins found in Sweden (in
his important description of Anglo-
Saxon coins in the Royal Swedish
Cabinet of Coins, Stockholm, 1844,
4to.) remarks, (says M. Worsaae,) 'that
along with them are generally found
silver ornaments, large rings for the
neck or the head, of wires twisted
together, smaller rings for the arm,
partly of wires twisted together, partly
of a single thin piece of silver the ends
of which form a beautiful knob; bracelets, sometimes with patterns which are
made with a punch, ingots both complete and broken, lumps of silver, most-

being adorned with inwrought triangular ornaments.   It
may be remarked in general, that these triangles are peculiar
to the majority of the ornaments of silver.

With regard to dress at this period we know little more of
a decided nature than we do of that of the bronze-period.
From the testimony of extant manuscripts it appears that it
usually consisted, in addition to the coverings of the head and
feet, of bræcan or breeches, a coat or robe, with its accompanying girdle, a mantle, and upper clothing of various kinds.
That these were formed sometimes of skins and sometimes of
woollen cloth[1] is established by discoveries which have been

ly hammered and rolled together for
convenience of transport, and in order
that they might be used as money.'
This description (remarks M. Worsaae)
would exactly apply to the silver ornaments found at Cuerdale. 'There can
be no doubt,' continues Hildebrand,
'that those ornaments, ingots, and
lumps of silver have accompanied the
coins from rich Asia, where they could
much more easily obtain silver than in
the northern parts of Europe, even if
we suppose that the little silver which
is to be found in the mines in the
Scandinavian mountains, was known
and used at the time in question.

This view is confirmed by the circumstance that similar ornaments are still
used in some parts of Asia.' "—T.

[1] Such was the case too in the British islands.

" In 1786 there was found, seventeen
feet below the surface of a bog in the
county of Longford," says Mr. Richard
Lovell Edgeworth, in his Report to the
Commissioners for improving the Bogs
in Ireland, (Appendix to Report II. p.
174), " a woollen coat of coarse but
even net-work, exactly in the form of
what is now called a spencer. It fitted
me as well as if it had been made by a
modern tailor. A razor (?) with a

made in barrows; and it is indubitable, that they often consisted of more costly materials, for instance of a sort of velvet, (peld,) which by means of trade, or Viking expeditions, was imported from other countries into the North.

We have thus investigated the swords and weapons with which our forefathers fought, in their distant expeditions by sea; we have become acquainted with the trinkets and ornaments which they admired; let us now cast a hasty glance over the drinking cups, which the heroes used at their banquets, when from the severity of the winter, or other causes, they were compelled to remain quietly at home. Over the cup they called to mind the gods and mighty heroes departed; over the cup they were excited to heroic actions, and pledged themselves to future warlike deeds; over the cup the future condition and the future fate of whole races of men, and even of entire kingdoms, was decided. The drinking cups, as may be supposed, were often costly, and wrought with much care.

That which is here figured is of silver, the ornamented margin of the mouth is of gold, while the foot is inlaid with small pieces of gold : the height is 4½ in., and the diameter of the mouth 4 in. Of glass, a material which was then so rare and so costly, there are found here and there cups and beakers, which in all probability were used at banquets, for the supposition that they were employed as urns to contain the ashes of the dead is very doubtful, on account of the smallness of their size. It is moreover beyond a doubt, that in ancient times there were drinking vessels of glass, in the

wooden handle, some iron heads of arrows, and large wooden bowls, some only half made, were also found, with the remains of turning tools; these were obviously the wreck of a work-shop, which was probably situate on the borders of a forest. The coat was presented by me to the Antiquarian Society."—T.

form of the horn of the ox. Ox-horns were the most usual drinking vessels, and thus it was said that the heroes in Walhalla should drink mead from horns. Similar to these, were the celebrated golden horns, which occupy so conspicuous a place among the antiquities found in the North. The first known example was exhumed in 1639, at Gallehuus, close to Mögeltondern, in the domain of Ribe. It consisted of a piece which was solid internally, round which were thirteen rings, seven of them loose, which were adorned with numerous images and figures. The horn was about two feet nine inches in length, the mouth four inches in diameter, and it weighed six pounds six ounces and a half, of the very finest gold. Almost a hundred years afterwards, namely in 1734, at the same village of Gallehuus, another golden horn was discovered, with one end broken off. It weighed seven pounds five ounces and a half, that is, fifteen ounces more than the former complete specimen. Like the former it was covered with ornamental rings, and it also bore round the mouth a heterogeneous inscription, in Runic characters. Unfortunately these invaluable rarities were stolen from the place in which they were preserved, and melted down, about forty years ago.

In connection with the drinking vessels have been found cullenders, and parts of bowls or large dishes, in which drink was handed round. They were either of metal, or of wood, with metal rings, handles, &c., of which the metallic portion alone remains[m].

[m] The accompanying engraving represents the remains of a bucket or vessel of such character, found in the right hand corner of a grave in a barrow in Bourne Park, the seat of Lord Albert Conyngham, in August,

It is a question which we are scarcely able to decide, whether these large gold horns, as well as several of the bowls which have been discovered, may not have been used in the sacrifices which our heathen forefathers practised in honour of their idols; and it is probable that the cakes of incense which are occasionally found with antiquities belonging to the times of heathenism, were also intended to be used in their religious ceremonies.

In conformity with facts which we derive from Sweden and Norway, it appears highly probable that the Danes erected idols in their places of worship. It is true no figures of them have hitherto been discovered, doubtless partly because they were in a great measure destroyed at the introduction of Christianity, when it is probable that the first preachers of Christianity exerted themselves to procure the destruction of the idols of paganism, partly too because they were of wood, and have perished in the earth. These idols were frequently adorned with costly garments, and trinkets of silver and gold. Hence a large massive ring or girdle of

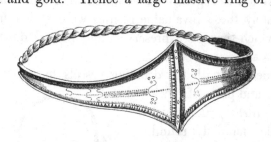

massive gold mixed with silver, which is rivetted together in the middle of the front, is conceived to have been the ornament of an idol, for it can scarcely be supposed that any

1844. The hoops, which were in perfect preservation, occupied their position one above another as if the wood had been there to support them. It appeared to have been about a foot high, the lower hoop was a foot in diameter, and the upper hoop exactly ten inches. The hooked feet would seem to have been intended to support the wood and prevent it from slipping. A somewhat similar vessel is represented in one of the plates of Douglas's Nenia.—T.

human being could constantly have worn such a ring, the
hinder part of which is also turned, and has a sharp edge.
With reference to its shape and ornaments, the ring, as the
engraving shews, displays a striking similarity with the armlet previously figured, (page 59). We must also enumerate
among the treasures originally appertaining to the temples of
their gods, certain massive gold rings, which are too small to
be worn round the head or the neck, while they do not seem
fitted to serve as rings for the wrist, since they end in two
large bosses or knobs, placed opposite to each other. Hence
it is possible, that these are the kind of rings which lay on
the altars, and were required to be touched by persons taking
an oath; and, yet, judging from their shape, this supposition
would appear doubtful and uncertain. The important and
costly nature of these rings may be estimated from the circumstance, that three rings of this kind, which in the year
1817 were found in a bed of gravel, in the field of the
village of Stotsbjergby, at Slagelse, weighed together thirty-
eight ounces, and were worth about £180; and that their
value must have been much greater in ancient times, when
the rich mines of America were still unknown to Europeans,
is perfectly obvious.

If we cast a glance over the varied objects of gold which
are here described, we shall at once perceive that Adam of
Bremen, who wrote about eight hundred years ago, spoke
the truth when he stated that gold and silver abounded to
excess in Seeland. Objects of gold are frequently discovered
in considerable quantities. At Broholm, in Fuhnen, a collection of trinkets was found, the weight of which was above
eight pounds; and it is a fact worthy of observation, that
they are usually found in level fields, in beds of gravel, in
short, where no barrows or elevations are to be seen. This
circumstance may perhaps be accounted for by the fact, that
the Vikings, when they undertook expeditions, buried their
treasures, that they might not be taken during their absence
either by foes or robbers; and then if they fell in battle,

or perished by any other means, no one knew where they had concealed their property. The most precious articles, it is true, were deposited in the barrows with the dead, but the greater part of such elevations in which articles of value occurred, were broken open and plundered in the middle ages.

The ancient writer above named farther mentions that the large quantity of gold existing in Seeland was obtained by piracy. This statement is to a certain degree correct; but it can scarcely be denied that many trinkets and ornaments were acquired by trade. The North was at an early period visited by merchants from southern countries, chiefly for the purpose of procuring amber and fur. In later times these commercial relations were extended farther, and from the North itself merchants sailed to distant countries, whence they brought home rare and costly wares. History, it is to be observed, does not afford us many particulars relating to this kind of life. The merchant did not stand in such high repute as the Viking, hence it was natural that the heroic deeds of the one should be described rather than the peaceful employments of the other. It is highly gratifying to observe how our antiquities afford in this respect important explanations, which serve both to confirm and to extend the materials of history.

In ancient times no money was coined in Denmark. Trade consisted, it is true, in a great degree, of exchange, but there were many instances in which it was necessary to have a kind of circulating medium. Instead of coins, pieces of silver and gold were used, which were cut off either from rings or bars, and passed according to their weight. Most commonly they made use of ring-silver, or of pieces of many different broken rings. It was not till about the year 1000, that King Svend Tveskiæg, the father of the Dano-Anglish King Cnut began to coin money in Denmark. Coined money however was frequently brought thither from southern regions, where civilization had made greater progress. This foreign money, which is here and there exhumed, is very important, and deserves particular attention, inasmuch as it not only serves to explain the commercial relations of antiquity, but often determines the age of other objects deposited with it; since the inscriptions which it bears can be referred to a positive period, which is seldom, if ever, the case with our other northern antiquities.

The oldest coins met with in Denmark are of Roman origin, and almost without exception date from 50 to 200 years after the birth of Christ. Of about the same period are 420 Roman coins, (from Tiberius to Marcus Aurelius,) which were dug up from a peat bog near Slagelse, towards the close of the last century. In other places also, for instance in Holstein, silver and copper coins of the same date have been found, but they occur most numerously in Bornholm. Roman imperial coins, which almost exclusively belong to those dates, are also met with in Sweden, but chiefly in Gothland and Oeland, as well as in the countries east and west of the Baltic, in Posen and in Poland, which seems to indicate that the connection which at that time existed between the Roman empire and the North originated and was kept up by means of the Roman possessions in Hungary. The fact that the coins belong to the period from 50 to 200 years after the birth of Christ may reasonably be explained by the circumstance that the Romans possessed fortified possessions in Hungary till about the close of the second century of the Christian era, for as early as the third century the Goths began to make incursions into the Roman empire, which from that time continued to lose more and more of its possessions, while it was torn both by external and internal wars. Amongst coins of the third and fourth century we find few if any Roman coins; nor was it till the division of the Roman empire into two portions, those of Eastern and Western Rome, which occurred about the year 400, that a connection with the eastern empire, whose capital was Byzantium, (Constantinople,) appears to have been opened.

The coins minted there, and which from this time were
brought to the North, were of gold, and were generally
called Byzants. In Denmark they occur chiefly of the fifth
and sixth centuries, and as has already been remarked, traces
occasionally exist of their having been fitted with a handle or
ring, and thus used as trinkets; the imitations of them, the
gold bracteates as they are called, have been already mentioned. It is obvious that the connection with Byzantium
must have lasted down to a somewhat late period, for the
Northmen, the Väringer as they were called, frequently repaired to Byzantium, where they took service in the emperor's
body-guard.

If we bear in mind that our forefathers belonged to the
great Gothic stock which wandered from the countries on
the Black and Caspian seas, we can easily explain why they
were both in connection with the Roman empire, and also
maintained a direct communication with the east. Proofs of
this latter fact are afforded by the numerous eastern coins
which are found in the North; they are chiefly of silver, and
being inscribed with the ancient Arabic character first introduced in the town of Cufa, are usually termed Cufic coins.
They occur in Denmark, most plentifully in Bornholm, where
in the time of Frederic IV., in cutting peat, a whole bushel
full was discovered. At Falster near Vaalse in the spring of
1835 was found a large deposit, consisting of about 160
pieces, in a vase of metal, together with many Anglo-Saxon
and German coins of the tenth century, bars and many
different trinkets of silver, with rings of twisted work, &c.,
which were partly broken, probably for the purpose of being
used in payment[n].

[n] The reader who will take the trouble to refer to Mr. Hawkins's "Account
of Coins and Treasure found in Cuerdale," in the Archæological Journal,
vol. iv. p. 110—130, cannot but be
struck with the resemblance between
this and the Cuerdale find, which consisted of a large mass of silver, consisting of ingots or bars of various sizes, a
few silver armlets tolerably entire, several fragments and a few ornaments, of
various kinds, cut into pieces of different dimensions and weights, amount-
ing to upwards of a thousand ounces,
exclusive of about six or seven thousand
coins, Anglo-Saxon, Cufic, &c.—T.

The Cufic coins hitherto found in the North were partly struck by the caliphs of Bagdad, partly by different princes, particularly the Samanides in Chorasan and Segestan, which were under their authority; they are all referrible to the period between the years 700 and 1050 after the birth of Christ. From the countries on the Caspian sea, in which the coins have almost all been struck, they must have been brought, with goods, as we must conjecture, up the Wolga, into the interior of Russia, to the important commercial town of Novogorod, which must have been founded by the Northmen. Here great markets were held, in which the traders of the North received eastern coins and rarities in return for their furs, dried fish, and amber. An active communication between Scandinavia and Asia was very generally maintained by way of northern Russia, (then termed Biarmiland and Garderica,) up to the conclusion of the eleventh century; when, in the first instance troubles in the interior of Russia, and subsequently the irruption of the Mongols, put a stop for some time to the usual progress of trade. Schleswig is mentioned by Arabian writers as an important commercial town, from whence many ships sailed to Russia. At Bornholm, where many Cufic coins are found, and at Gothland it is said the travellers to Russia assembled for their journey. Gothland, judging from the innumerable Cufic coins which have been dug up there, together with silver articles, and Anglo-Saxon and German coins of the tenth and eleventh centuries, must have been even in the heathen period, the most important place in the North for its commercial intercourse with the east by way of Russia, as well as with Germany and England. It was by means of this commerce that the town of Wisby° attained in later times to its extraordinary height of power and riches.

° Of the town of Wisby, so interesting to antiquaries from its connection with the early commerce of Europe, —it having been perhaps the greatest place for trade in northern Europe,— and from the manner in which its ancient buildings are preserved, a slight historical sketch was published

As the coins afford us an insight into the relations of our
forefathers towards the east, so they give us also important
hints as to the connection of the North with the west of
Europe. It is a fact, established beyond all doubt, that the
inhabitants of the North carried on trade with the countries
of the west; but at the close of paganism, this connection
assumed more and more of a warlike character, and instead
of peaceful merchants vast hordes of rude Vikings landed on
their coasts. Numerous English and Dutch coins of the tenth
and eleventh centuries which are met with here in the North,
sufficiently testify the fortunate expeditions of the Northmen
to the west; and in modern times coins have been discovered
which were probably struck by leaders of bands of Vikings.
Thus among others a coin has been found which bears on one
side the head of the French king, Charles the Bald, while the
reverse presents the name of a northern Sea king Cnut. On
another coin, also of Cnut, is the name of the English king
Alfred the Great. Cnut must therefore have visited both
England and France in his expeditions. Some of the coins are
only inscribed with a northern name; for instance the coins
of King Sigfred, who was probably the same with that King
Sigfred who with his Northmen, according to the testimony
of old chroniclers, made important conquests in France, and
was particularly distinguished for his daring attacks on Paris.
These and other similar coins serve in an important degree
to confirm and to explain the statements of the chronicles as
to the expeditions of the northern Vikings into the west of
Europe.

Since foreign valuables and wares must infallibly have been
introduced with foreign coins, we have consequently, with
reference to the antiquities of the iron-period, to determine
between 1. The purely Roman or antique objects; 2. The
east Roman or Byzantine; 3. The eastern; 4. Those derived from western Europe; and lastly, 5. Those of which it

by Professor Soderberg in 1845, under   ner, jemte Förord om Gothland och
the title of " Vägledare i Wisby Rui-   Wisby," &c. Wisby, 1845.—T.

is to be assumed that they have their origin in the North itself.

Among the purely Roman antiquities must be comprised most of the large vessels of metal, and in particular some round turned vessels with handles, together with cullenders, some glass objects, &c. In a gravel-pit at Nörre Broby in Fühnen, in the spring of 1839, among several vessels of metal, hair-pins, beads, spurs, &c., was found a small round mirror, made of a mixture of zinc and other metal, resembling exactly what are decided to be Roman mirrors, together with the remains of the handle of a vessel on which was inscribed the stamp of a Roman manufactory. With the coins of eastern Rome golden trinkets adorned with crescent-shaped ornaments wrought in the material are occasionally found, which trinkets possibly have been introduced with the coins. From the East too in all probability came the objects of silver, for not merely in Denmark, but also in other countries of the North, the twisted silver rings, and other silver trinkets, which sometimes have triangular ornaments, are almost always found associated with Cufic coins. To point out with decision what objects have been introduced from the west of Europe to the North, would be attended with much difficulty, although on account of the numerous Viking expeditions the number of such objects must doubtless have been very considerable. At the same time it is perfectly clear that the ornaments which characterize the iron-period, have by no means been originated in the North; since they bear the greatest similarity to the ornaments on cotemporary Anglo-Saxon and Frankish works. There is also good reason to suppose, that the higher degree of civilization which prevailed at an earlier period towards the west, in England, France, and in the countries of the south, and which had arisen on the ruins of the by-gone civilization of Rome, exercised an important influence on the development of the ruder nations of the North.

The characteristic ornaments of the iron-period are symmetrical windings and arabesques. These symmetrical winding

ornaments are not only introduced into
trinkets, as in the bracteate here figured, but
into most other works of the same period,
for instance in the handles of swords, (see
the figure p. 49); and even on the Runic
stones, where the inscription is frequently
inclosed within ornaments of this nature.

As they not unfrequently terminate in a rude representation
of the head of some fantastic animal, these symmetrical winding ornaments have been regarded as the figures of snakes,
whence they are called snake ornaments. It must however
be observed, that these embellishments are copied from an
ancient Roman taste; and that the fanciful heads of animals
chiefly occupy the place of what were originally leaves, and
that from the very first no attempt was made to give an
exact representation of any particular animal. For this reason
we cannot maintain that a dragon is figured on the cup

here depicted, or name the embellishments
snake ornaments; they are merely symmetrical turns and arabesques, with the usual
fantastic heads of animals. The cup here
mentioned is of silver, and about an inch
and three quarters high; it was taken from
the grave of the celebrated Queen Thyre

Danebod, at Jellinge; we therefore know decidedly that it
dates from the tenth century. The reverse of the great
Runic stone at Jellinge, which in the same century King
Harald Blaatand erected in honour of his parents Gorm and
Thyre, is adorned with similar ornaments; and it is a fact
which is confirmed by many examples, that symmetrical windings and arabesques continued in the North long after the
introduction of Christianity.

Although the arts during the iron-period were chiefly
confined to the imitation of the trinkets and valuables of
other countries, yet in this respect they probably attained no
mean degree of excellence. It is at the same time very pos-

sible that many objects which we regard as foreign, were actually manufactured in Denmark; for not only are able smiths mentioned in our ancient records, but it is also self-evident that a people who were in active communication with other countries, where civilization had made greater advances, and who could build ships with which the Vikings were enabled to undertake many and distant voyages, must have learned to manufacture trinkets and other objects of comfort and luxury, when at a later period such great riches were brought to the North by the expeditions of the Vikings.

It has already been shewn in the previous pages, that Antiquities from the stone and bronze-period occur very plentifully in Denmark, and the south-west part of the present Sweden, but very rarely or only in single specimens in the other parts of Sweden, and the whole of Norway. With regard to the objects from the iron-period the circumstances are wholly reversed. The swords and other weapons characteristic of that period, the oval clasps for the breast, the mosaic beads, &c., are so common in Sweden and Norway, that traces of them are discovered in nearly every barrow which has been examined there; on the contrary, in Denmark (with the exception of Bornholm, which in an antiquarian point of view is connected with Sweden) they occur but very rarely indeed, when compared with the objects of stone and bronze. In places of historical note for instance, as Leire and Jellinge, which we must consider as having been tolerably well peopled in the pagan times, swords and trinkets belonging almost exclusively to the bronze-period alone have been exhumed; but none from the iron-period, although numerous graves in the neighbourhood have been opened. This can scarcely be a matter of accident, since the Royal Museum of Northern Antiquities in Copenhagen, which during a series of years has received accessions from different parts of the country, and from many hundred barrows, possesses only a very few weapons of iron, which are known to have been found in heathen graves; while, on the other hand, it exhibits several hundred swords and daggers of the bronze-period.   If it should be objected that the soil of Denmark may destroy objects of iron sooner than that of Norway and Sweden, it must be observed that Wendish weapons of iron are frequently discovered in heathen graves in Mecklenburg, the soil of which country is similarly constituted to that of Denmark. It must also be remarked that not only the iron weapons but also the other antiquities of the iron-period, such as brass brooches, beads, and ornaments of stone and glass, are exceedingly scarce in Denmark, so that if it be admitted that the iron weapons have been corroded, we should have full reason to expect to find the ornaments of brass, stone, and glass, remaining.   It has also been maintained that iron from its costliness and value was not deposited in graves, as was the case with bronze.   But was not bronze as costly, and in fact more so, since it consisted of two metals melted together, one of which, tin, could not have been procured at any place nearer than England.   It is also well known that while no copper exists here, the soil of Denmark affords, in single spots, iron ore, which the water of the meadows and of the lakes has separated, and which at a later period of history has been smelted by the peasants.   The want of objects of the iron-period in Denmark can moreover scarcely be satisfactorily explained, unless we acknowledge that the art of smelting iron ore, like the civilization of the iron-period generally, must have reached Denmark later than the other parts of the North, where iron occurs in infinitely greater masses.   This circumstance appears to be confirmed, both by the nature of the barrows, and by the progress of the peopling of Scandinavia, which subject will be discussed in a future page.   A comprehensive consideration of the antiquities in the different countries of the North, taken as a whole, will plainly shew that the three northern kingdoms have by no means been subject to the same alterations in civilization during the periods of the past.

It remains only to be remarked that Christianity was not finally established in Scandinavia until the eleventh century, and consequently, that the primeval Antiquities extend to that period.

SECOND DIVISION.

OF STONE STRUCTURES, BARROWS, &c.

To obtain correct ideas on the subject of the first peopling and the most ancient relations of our native country, it will not be sufficient to direct attention exclusively to objects exhumed from the earth. It is at the same time indispensably necessary to examine and compare with care the places in which antiquities are usually found; otherwise many most important collateral points can either not be explained at all, or at least in a very unsatisfactory manner. Thus we should scarcely have been able to refer, as we have done in the previous pages, the antiquities to three successive periods, if experience had not taught us that objects which belong to different periods are usually found by themselves. It is not however all places where objects are discovered which will here be treated of in a similar manner. For instance a great number of antiquities are found in peat-bogs, but who could safely maintain that such articles had lain there ever since the period when they were generally used, and have not been mingled at a later period with more modern objects lost or thrown in there. It will not be the places where antiquities may be casually met with, but rather our ancient stone structures and barrows, which, with reference to the subject just mentioned, ought to be the subject of a more particular description; for as to the graves themselves we know that, generally speaking, they contain both the bones of the dead, and many of their weapons, implements, and trinkets, which were buried with them. Here we may therefore, in general, expect to find those objects together which were originally used at the same period. The barrows serve to explain in various other ways the associations of pagan antiquity. They afford the surest guides to a knowledge of funeral ceremonies which gradually became dissimilar to each other, and since they are fixed and lasting memorials which may be destroyed altogether, but cannot be transferred from their original place, their situation and extension furnish us with very important testimony as to the most ancient settlement and occupancy of different districts. From a single mound standing by itself, we must not of course attempt to deduce too much, but by comparing a number of observations from all parts of the country, we arrive, by degrees, at a knowledge of the general and particular characteristics of the grave, and by this mean learn to refer the different kinds to distinct classes, and in some measure to distinct periods. Experience of this kind is of high value and importance. For, to cite an example, if we can prove that there exist in certain districts, barrows and structures of stone of the same form and the same contents, and that, beyond these districts, other and opposite relations exist, we certainly have a valid reason for concluding that such districts were inhabited in ancient times either by the same races of men, or at all events by races very nearly related.

The barrows of Denmark, Norway, and Sweden, like the antiquities of these countries, were at an earlier time all considered as belonging to one class, so that monuments of the most different kind were mixed together, as if they belonged to one period. For this reason we will just point out very briefly the chief classes of the acknowledged Danish monuments, and afterwards examine their connection with the ancient remains which exist in other parts of the North.

The Danish grave-hills are, like the early antiquities, generally divisible into three classes, namely, those of the stone, of the bronze, and that of the iron-period, which last includes the inscribed monumental stones, or Runic stones, as they are termed.

GRAVES OF THE STONE-PERIOD, OR CROMLECHS, (STEENDYSSER.)

The important and highly ancient memorials which are usually termed Cromlechs in England, Steingräber in Germany, and often Urgräber, (ancient graves, or Hünengräber, giants' graves,) are slightly elevated mounds surrounded by a number of upright stones, on the top of which are erected chambers formed of large stones placed one upon the other. Although many of them have been removed or destroyed for the sake of the stones, they still exist in Denmark in very considerable numbers. They are most frequently met with on the coast, particularly on the north and west coast of Seeland, on the coasts of Fühnen, in the north of Jütland at the Lümfiord, particularly in the domain of Thisled, as well as along the east coasts of Jütland, Sleswig, and Holstein. They occur more rarely on the west coasts, and still more seldom in the interior of the country. They may be divided into two chief kinds; 1st the long, and 2nd the small round Cromlechs, (Langdysser og Runddysser.) The term Cromlech is here applied not only to the stone chamber, but to the whole monument. As the long cromlechs (one of which we here

figure as it is seen sideways) exist in great quantities in various districts of the country, their size is naturally very different. For the most part they are from sixty to a hundred and twenty feet in length, occasionally somewhat smaller, but there are instances of their being two hundred, and in some few cases four hundred feet in length. Their breadth on the other hand is very inconsiderable, at most they are only from sixteen to twenty-four, and the very longest of all thirty to forty feet.

No general rule can be stated as to the direction in which they lie. They are most frequently met with from east to west, they also lie from south to north, and from north-east to south-west. The aborigines do not seem to have confined themselves to any precise rule in the erection of such monuments.

Peculiar care and industry have been bestowed on enclosing these elevations with large stones. Occasionally one descries above a hundred colossal blocks of stone, set round the foot of a hill in an elongated circle, and this too in districts where not only in the present day, but also without a doubt in ancient times, there was a deficiency of such stones. There are also traces in some instances of the hill having been originally surrounded with two or more large enclosures of stone.

The stone chambers[p] erected on the summit of these mounds

of earth are formed of a roofing or cap-stone which rests on several supporting stones placed in a circle.

[p] The accompanying woodcut exhibits the south view of a small cromlech at L'ancresse in the Island of Guernsey, described in Mr. Lukis' curi-

ous paper 'On the Primeval Antiquities of the Channel Islands,' printed in the Third No. of the Archæological Journal, pp. 222—233. Several stone hammers and arrow-points were found in it in the year 1838, as also some portions of earthen vessels, the latter being in several instances of a finer description than that discovered in the large cromlech on the hill near to it.—T.

The cap-stone is often from thirty to forty feet in circumference, and eight to ten feet in length, the side of it which is turned underneath, and forms the roof of the chamber, has always a smooth flat surface, while the side turned uppermost is almost always of a very irregular form. The supporting stones are also flat only on the side which is turned to the chamber. They commonly fit close to each other, the small openings which, from the nature of the material, may occur between them, being stopped up with flat pieces of stone placed one upon the other. The usual height of the supporting stones is from six to eight feet, and their breadth from two to three feet; their number depends on the height of the chamber; they are usually from four to five, but occasionally about fifteen have been met with in one of those structures; whence it follows that such a chamber must have had more than one roofing stone. The floor of the chamber itself is paved partly with flat stones, and partly with a number of small flints which appear to have been exposed to a very powerful heat. The chambers are either quite round, from five to seven feet in diameter, or they are oval and from twelve to sixteen feet in length, or they are merely formed of their supporting stones, so placed, that the two longest form the side walls and the shortest the cap-stone at the end.

Entrances of regular form, enclosed with blocks of stone, provided with a roof, and leading to the chambers of the long cromlechs, are very rare and are met with only in the largest of them. There is in general an opening between two of the supporting stones, which is sometimes indicated externally by two flat stones placed upright, or occasionally by a row of stones placed along the side of the hill and leading to such entrance. Like the hill itself there is no rule as to the direction in which it is placed; in most cases it has a direction south and east, and occasionally south-east, south-west, and north.

The most important of these monuments are the long cromlechs, which consist of three chambers, a large one in the middle and a small one at each end. Stone structures with two chambers occur most frequently and present no particular form. On the other hand it is very remarkable that in those which have but one chamber, it is usually placed at one end, even when the barrows are of considerable length. Thus at the Clelund field in the district of Lindknud, in the domain of Ribe, there exists a stone enclosure which is about three hundred and seventy feet in length, in which however the stone chamber is situated only forty feet from the south-west end.

A great number of these chambers have been opened and explored, probably in most cases by persons who hoped to find great treasure in them. They are therefore frequently found quite exposed, although originally they were no doubt covered with earth, yet only in such a manner as to leave a portion of the stones which formed the roof visible. Of these cromlechs there are many still remaining. The chambers formed the regular place of interment, in which several bodies probably of the same family were deposited. We are not however to conceive that the space was ever left empty. As soon as a corpse had been deposited in it, it appears to have been filled with earth or clay and pebbles firmly trodden down, and not to have been opened until a new corpse was to be interred. In examining such sepulchral chambers as have remained undisturbed until the present time, it has been ascertained that they always contained the skeletons of one or more bodies, together with arrow-heads, lances, chisels, and axes of flint, implements of bone, ornaments of amber or of bone, and earthen vessels filled with loose earth. Even in the chambers which now remain open, and bear evident traces of having been before explored, we meet, on thorough investigation, with pieces of earthen vessels, single stone implements, and human bones, which plainly shew that these chambers do not preserve their original form, but that they were applied to the same purpose as those which are still partially covered with earth.

The small circular cromlechs differ from those above described only in the circumstance that the elevations are much

smaller, and usually comprise but one chamber, which however with reference to its size is seldom inferior to the
chambers of the oblong cromlechs⁹. At the same time it
has been observed that the cap-stones of the small round cromlechs usually rest on five supporting stones.

The round cromlechs have been preserved in greater number than those previously described, but it is evident that
they have been erected solely for the same purposes. Excavations have led to exactly the same results', since the

ᵐ The accompanying woodcut, for
which we are indebted to Mr. Lukis'

paper already mentioned, represents a
round cromlech at Catiroc in the Island

of Guernsey, called the Trepid; a name,
as Mr. Lukis well remarks, "sufficiently
modern, to denote the loss of its original appellation." This cromlech was
covered by three or four cap-stones, the
principal of which remains in its place,
the others have fallen in; and in the interior were found urns, human bones,
and flint arrow-heads.—T.

ʳ The accompanying engraving re-

presents the interior of the cromlech at L'ancresse, in the northern part
of Guernsey, explored by that intelligent observer, Mr. Lukis, in 1837, and
described by him in the first vol. of
the Archæological Journal. From this
cromlech about forty urns of different
sizes, some being 18 and some not
more than 4 inches in height, were obtained; "but," adds Mr. Lukis, "from

chambers of the small cromlechs likewise contain unburnt human bones, articles of stone and amber, as well as earthen vessels [s]. As the mounds on which they are raised were

the quantity of pottery found therein, not fewer than one hundred varieties

Silt sand.

Brown sand.

Rubbish, &c. with Animal bones

Deposits of shells, human bones, pottery and jars.

of vessels must have been deposited from time to time during the primeval period."—T.

[s] Remains of a precisely similar character have been found in this country :

and the following engraving represents portions of a trough and some stone hammers, quoits, and other implements found in the cromlech at L'ancresse, described by Mr. Lukis, and the next

considerably smaller than those of the long graves, and therefore easier to remove, the chambers in most cases are either
accessible or open altogether.   But even in the floor of these
we constantly find either very ancient graves but slightly
disturbed, or undoubted remains of these, as human bones,
broken vessels of clay, and objects of stone and amber.

We have already mentioned in the Introduction that the
erroneous opinion which regarded the stone utensils as sacrificial instruments, also transformed cromlechs, and the hills on
which they were constructed, into places of judgment, altars
of sacrifice, and sacred abodes of the gods.   The idea that
the antiquities of stone were instruments of sacrifice is now
indeed pretty generally rejected, but the opinion that the
cromlechs raised by our forefathers were intended for places
of judgment, or for altars, is still occasionally maintained.
It will therefore be necessary to enquire further, as briefly as
possible, how far that opinion may be well founded.

The idea entertained is as follows; the long cromlechs
were places of worship at which the people assembled to
consult on their common affairs, to decide differences, &c. &c.;
on the large surrounding stones sat the judges and the elders
of the people, and sacrifices were offered to the idols on the
chambers of stone or altars.   These sacrifices, it is thought,

exhibits the position of one of the   it was surrounded by animal remains,
vases alluded to in the preceding   chiefly bones of the horse, and of the
note as having been discovered in the   ox, and tusks of the boar.—T.
same locality ; and the manner in which

were conducted as follows : the victim was placed on the roof of the stone chamber, and when slain, the blood, from which the sacrificing priest derived his auguries, flowed into the chamber or opening under the cap-stone.

A cursory glance at the exterior arrangement of the cromlech will, it is conceived, suffice to shew that it is as utterly unfit for a place of judgment, (since the surrounding blocks of stone could never have afforded suitable seats,) as it is for an altar. If we adopt the latter supposition, the cap-stones must be sufficiently flat to admit of the animals intended to be sacrificed resting upon them. It is however a rule, without exception, that the flat side, instead of being uppermost, is invariably turned towards the chamber; beside which, we have also seen, that, with the view of guarding the chamber and its contents, the supporting stones were placed close to each other, while the interstices were filled with fragments which rendered it perfectly impossible for the blood of the sacrifice to flow from the cap-stone into the chamber. Again, the situation in which the cromlechs are met with plainly shews that they were neither altars nor seats of justice. They are found chiefly on the coast and in distinct districts; for instance in the parish of Rachlov near Kallundborg there are more than a hundred of these long and round cromlechs, while in Jellinga and other well-known parishes of very remote antiquity we do not meet with a single monument of this kind, a fact which is quite inconsistent with the idea of such monuments being altars or places of judgment. Moreover, it would be extremely singular if the first Christians, who sought with so much zeal to destroy every trace of heathenism, should have allowed these offensive altars of sacrifice to have been preserved. Let us add, that these altars, as they are termed, never occur either in Norway or in the northern part of Sweden, where paganism prevailed until the latest period; and finally, that, in general, human bones and funereal objects are exhumed from them, so that we can safely maintain that they are merely graves appertaining to the most ancient time, and that for this reason they usually occur on the coast.

GIANTS' CHAMBERS (JÆTTESTUER.)

The view here expressed as to the origin and nature of the cromlechs acquires greater force and clearness from the circumstance that stone chambers perfectly corresponding to these, but on a somewhat larger scale, are frequently discovered, forming places of interment within large barrows of earth raised by the hands of man. These tombs, covered with earth, have perhaps contained the remains of the powerful and the rich. They are almost all provided with long entrances which lead from the exterior of the mound of earth to the east or south side of the chambers. For this reason it has been proposed to call these structures "passage buildings," (Gang bygningen). The entrances, like the chambers, are formed of large stones, smooth on the side which is turned inwards, on which very large roof-stones are placed. As a single chamber is therefore formed of a considerable number of heavy masses of stone, which would be extremely difficult to set up, independently of placing them on one another, it is highly probable that the name of "Giants' Chambers" may have had its origin in the opinion of the lower classes, that the giants (jætter) who, according to the Sagas, could with ease hurl enormous rocks, were alone able to execute such stupendous works[t].

[t] The reader will find much curious illustration of the connection which exists, in the minds of the common people, between the giants of popular mythology and the monuments we are considering, in that storehouse of Folklore, Grimm's Deutsche Mythologie, (ed. 1844,) p. 500, et seq. He will there see how works formerly ascribed to the giants have, since the introduction of Christianity, been attributed to Satanic agency. While on this subject, it may be remarked, that the name of giants' chambers, proposed by Mr. Worsaae, has its counterpart in the name generally bestowed upon cromlechs in the south-east of Ireland, where they are commonly designated giants' graves or beds; while in the north and west they are called beds of Dermot and Graine, *Leaba Diarmada agus Graine*, from a legend very current through the country of their having been erected by Dermot O' Duibhne, with whom

The giants' chambers, like the chambers of the cromlechs, are round or oval. In those tumuli which contain round chambers, two such have several times been found near each other, each with a separate entrance. Those which are circular are from five to eight feet in diameter, and about that height. A grown man can usually stand upright in the apartment, when the earth with which it is filled is removed. For these chambers, and even the entrances, which are from sixteen to twenty feet in length, are filled with trodden earth and pebbles, the object of which doubtless was to protect the repose of the dead in their grave. The same objects are discovered in these giant chambers as are found in the cromlechs, namely, unburnt skeletons, which were occasionally placed in sand on a pavement of flat or round stones, together with implements and weapons and tools of flint or bone, ornaments, pieces of amber, and urns of clay. Skeletons are also occasionally found deposited in the passages leading to the giant chambers ; a circumstance which may be explained by supposing that such giant chambers were sometimes family burial-places, which were filled as the members of the family died : and that when the chambers themselves could contain no more bodies, recourse was necessarily had to the entrance. That these giant chambers have been opened, from time to time, is evident from the fact that in general they are found to contain a quantity of fragments of broken pottery, which had been broken at some remote period.

The largest and most considerable of the giants' chambers are the long ones, which are from sixteen to twenty-four feet in length and from six to eight feet in breadth[u]. The en-

Graine, the wife of Finn Mac Coul, eloped. Finn set out in pursuit of the fugitives, but they escaped for a year and a day, during which time they never slept in the same bed for more than one night. Hence the number of these in Ireland was 366, according to the legend. See Mr. Wakeman s

excellent little "Hand-Book of Irish Antiquities, Pagan and Christian," p. 12.—T.

[u] The annexed cut, from the Journal of the Archaeological Association, (vol. i. p. 26,) shews the position of the stones, and the form of the cromlech Du Tus, or De Hus, when it was

trance is generally about twenty feet long. By some writers they are styled by the less striking epithet of semi-cruciform graves.

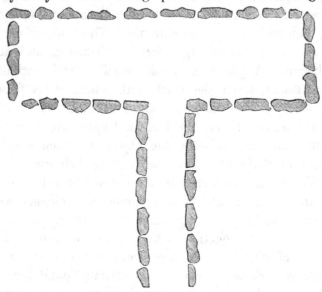

examined in 1837. The outer circle of stones is about sixty feet in diameter, and the total length of the chamber nearly forty feet from east to west.—T.

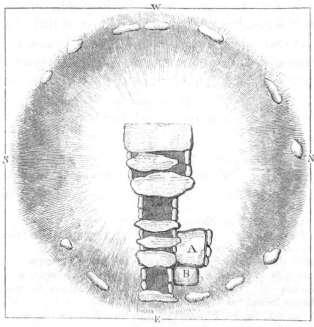

With reference to their contents and their general arrangements they entirely accord with the circular giant chambers; while as a natural consequence of their increased length, they contain a greater quantity of human remains. Meantime the manner in which the deceased were interred deserves peculiar attention, because by such means no unimportant light is thrown on the funeral customs which prevailed at the period. Thus along the sides of the stones forming the walls are found the bones of a number of bodies, which certainly cannot have been placed in the usual recumbent posture, for the space would not admit of it. On the contrary, the position of the remains seems to indicate that the bodies were placed in a compressed or sitting posture; by which means, the advantage of depositing many of them in a small space was obtained[x]. This is peculiarly evident in the single

[x] The accompanying engravings, derived from the communications of Mr. Lukis, afford remarkable illustrations of the prevalence of this custom.

The first, from the Archæological Journal, vol. i. p. 146, represents the interior of a cromlech situate on the summit of a gentle hill standing in the plain of L'Ancresse, in the northern parts of Guernsey. The second woodcut, (from the Journal of the Archæological Association, vol. i. p. 27,) which is yet more strikingly corroborative of the accuracy of Mr. Worsaae's statement, exhibits the posture of two skeletons in a vertical kneeling position, discovered in 1844, in the chamber of the cromlech Du Tus, which is marked B in the

giants' chambers, which were divided into small quadrangular spaces, one for each separate corpse.

In all probability the bodies were placed in the same manner in the circular giants' chambers and in the cromlechs; for the dimensions of the chambers are often so limited that a man of the usual height could not be laid at full length in them.

Of the heaped-up giants' chambers several have been preserved in an uninjured state. Thus in North Seeland the Ullershöi at Smidstrup, in the domain of Fredriksborg, with two chambers; the Julianahöi at Jagersprüs, the well-known giants' chambers at Oppesundbye, Udleire and Oehm in the neighbourhood of Roeskilde; again at Möen; the Röd-

woodcut already inserted, (vide note u, p. 88.) On the removal of the capstones, the upper part of two human skulls were exposed to view. One was facing the north, and the other the south, but both disposed in a line from

east to west. As the examination proceeded downwards into the interior, the bones of the extremities became exposed to view and seen to greater advantage. They were less decomposed than those of the upper part. The teeth and jaws, which were well preserved, denoted that they were the skeletons of adults, and not of old men. —T.

dingehöi with two giants' chambers; in Jütland in the domain
of Thisted near Ullerup, in the parish of Heltborg, in the so-
termed Lundhill an oval giants' chamber, (twenty-four feet
long, about five feet and a half broad, and four feet and a half

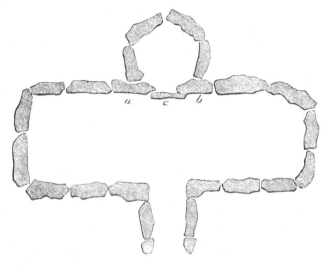

high,) inside of which is a smaller round chamber (six feet in
diameter and three feet and a half high.)   This grave is not
only remarkable for its peculiar form, but also from the circumstance that the two stones a and b, which stand on each
side of the threshold c, contain on the flat surface several
markings very faintly carved or rubbed in, which by some are
regarded as a species of Runic inscription.   These chambers
were first discovered in 1837, but as nothing was discovered
in the oval and largest of them, it is highly probable that the
barrow had been opened and examined at an earlier period,
from which the origin of the above-mentioned markings may
perhaps be dated.   It must not be overlooked in this respect,
that in Seeland, at Herresup, in the Odsherred, there has been
discovered, in a barrow, a chamber, on the roof of which
some figures very faintly carved have also been traced.   As
some of these are similar to markings on stones in Sweden
and Norway, which certainly are to be ascribed to the later
periods of paganism, and which are also only found on the

outside of the roofing stones, we can only suppose that they date from a later period than that in which the stone chamber (which, as usual, contained only implements of stone) was originally constructed. This however is a circumstance which at present can scarcely be determined with sufficient certainty, and will be better left to future and closer investigation.

An examination of the most remarkable and striking cromlechs and giants' chambers, cannot fail to excite our surprise that the aboriginal inhabitants of Denmark were able to erect such stupendous monuments. How the large cap-stones were brought to lie on the supporting stones is indeed not quite incomprehensible. It might have been effected by forming steep paths or inclined planes composed of earth and stems of trees, from the upper part of the supporting stones to the surface of the surrounding field, and by forcing the stones up these paths by means of levers. It may also be added that possibly the inhabitants had been able to tame and employ the horse, which must have existed in the country from the earliest period. It is still more remarkable if, being destitute of tools of metal, they were in a situation so to split the large roofing and supporting masses of stone, that they are completely flat on the side which is turned towards the chamber. For it is highly probable that many or most of them have been artificially split. Their number is too great to allow of the supposition that they all possess the natural form, whilst it is quite evident that the small flat fragments which fill up the interstices between the supporting stones have been split by artificial means. Hence it is possible that the aborigines were acquainted with the simple method of splitting large blocks of granite, which is still practised in several countries. Holes bored in a certain direction along the veins of the stone are filled with water. Wedges are then introduced into these holes, and struck with heavy mallets till the rock is split into two flat pieces. It must of course be supposed in this case that the aborigines knew how, by means of other stones, to form these holes or perforations in the granite, but this supposition is by no means incredible. Under all circumstances, this much is certain, that the cromlechs and giants' chambers must have been works of enormous labour; they therefore afford a striking proof, that the earliest inhabitants of Denmark could scarcely have led a mere nomadic life, but must have had settled habitations, and that they were a vigorous people who cherished care and reverence for the departed; a trait which is the more admirable, since they were in other respects rude, and destitute of any thing like regular civilization.

II. Tombs of the Bronze-period.

The barrows, cromlechs, and giants' graves of the stone-period, and the barrows of the bronze-period, are totally different from each other. The tombs of the stone-period are peculiarly distinguished by their important circles of stones and large stone chambers, in which are found the remains of unburnt bodies, together with objects of stone and amber. Those of the bronze-period, on the other hand, have no circles of massive stones, no stone chambers, in general no large stones on the bottom, with the exception of stone cists placed together, which however are easily to be distinguished from the stone chambers; they consist, as a general rule, of mere earth, with heaps of small stones, and always present themselves to the eye as mounds of earth which, in a few very rare instances are surrounded by a small circle of stones, and contain relics of bodies which have been *burned and placed in vessels of clay with objects of metal.*

From the fact that bodies during the bronze-period were burned, it may be conceived that the bronze-period is later than the stone-period, in which it was the general custom to bury the dead without burning. This latter method of interment is peculiar to uncultivated nations, and is unquestionably the most simple and the most natural; the custom of burning the dead supposes a certain developement of religious feeling which is only to be found among such nations as have acquired some degree of civilization. It was a totally different matter however, when towards the close of paganism in the North, cultivation having attained a higher grade, men once more adopted the custom of interring their dead without first burning them. This fact by no means invalidates the assertion, that the mode of interment of the stone-period is the most ancient. That the stone-period extends farthest into antiquity, the tombs which belong to it afford the most unquestionable proofs. At the summit and on the sides of a barrow are often found vessels of clay with burnt bones and articles of bronze, while at the base of the hill we meet with the ancient cromlechs or giants' chambers, with unburnt bodies and objects of stone. From this it is obvious that at a later time, possibly centuries after, poorer persons who had not the means to construct barrows, used the ancient tombs of the stone-period, which they could do with the more security, since a barrow which is piled above a giant's chamber had exactly the same appearance as a barrow of the bronze-period. To prevent misunderstanding it must here be observed, that many persons are of opinion, from the appearance of the barrows when opened, that the different modes of interment of the periods of stone and bronze, the placing bodies in cromlechs and the burning them, prevailed universally at one and the same time. This opinion has however been founded in most cases on very loose grounds, since sufficient attention has not been paid to distinguishing the different modes of interment at the base and the summit of the barrows; for the fact that two kinds of interment occur in the same barrow, by no means proves that such interments belong to the same era. The circumstance moreover that together with unburnt bodies vessels of clay have also been found, in the cromlechs and giants' chambers, has given rise to error. These vessels contain, as we have seen, merely loose earth; but formerly it was constantly as erroneously conceived, that all vessels of clay found in barrows were urns for ashes, and had been filled with

burnt human bones. We are certainly not justified in positively denying, that burnt human bones have ever been found
in a legitimate grave of the stone-period, but experience has
hitherto shewn us that between the tombs of the stone-period
and those of the bronze-period, there exists a difference as
great, and in fact greater, than that which prevails between
the antiquities of the two periods.

The usual mode of interment in the bronze-period appears
to have been as follows. A large pile of wood was erected,
on which the body was placed. When the pile was consumed, the small bones which remained were collected together with some portion of the surrounding ashes, and placed
in an earthen vessel, which was deposited in the midst of the
consumed pile and surrounded with stones. In this vessel,
in addition to the bones and the ashes, were deposited different small articles of bronze, such as pins, knives, pincers,
&c., and together with these the various weapons and ornaments possessed by the deceased. After this the vessel was
carefully closed with its usual cover, or, more generally, with
a flat stone; the whole was then covered with small stones,
which were usually placed in a conical heap, over which the
usual barrow of earth was erected. Instead of urns for ashes,
very small stone cists about a foot long, formed of four stones
placed together, and covered with a fifth, were occasionally used.
It is generally speaking characteristic of this period, that the
remains of burnt bodies were placed in no definite way and
in no definite parts of the hill. In the midst of the consumed
pile, the sword and the ornaments of the deceased were occasionally placed, covered with a heap of stones thrown over
them, while the urn with the ashes was deposited in the earth
which was placed upon them. On the floor of some of these
barrows the weapons are preserved in small oval cists of stone,
and again in others nothing is found but single portions of
bone, while the urns with ashes are placed outside. On the
very margin of the hill bronze swords and other weapons, as
well as ornaments, are met with, among loose burnt bones,

which are not collected in urns, but merely surrounded with small stones. Most of the barrows of this period were family-barrows, serving as places of interment for single families. Hence not only may the floor of a barrow be furnished with a great number of urns, or small stone cists filled with bones, but it is also very common, particularly on the east and south sides, and scarcely a foot in depth below the turf, to find numerous urns surrounded with stones which unquestionably have been deposited from time to time. The number of them, often from thirty to seventy, probably results from the circumstance of many poor persons having by degrees deposited their urns in the barrows of the rich. Since cinerary urns are not unfrequently dug up both in open fields and in beds of peat, the poorer classes have probably been obliged to select this simple mode of interment because they had no opportunity of placing the ashes of their relatives in a barrow.

A remarkable barrow with peculiar contents was examined in 1827, at the village of Vollerslev, in the neighbourhood of Aabenraa (Apenrade). On the removal of the earth, on the south side of the barrow, there was found, above the surface of the surrounding field, a small cinerary urn of clay, and below this a heap of small stones, thrown together. On the removal of these, a very thick stem of an oak, about ten feet in length and split in two, was discovered, which was rough-hewn and bore the marks of a saw. The upper part was found to be the cover of a cist hollowed out in the oak stem, six feet long, and nearly two broad[y]. In it was found a mantle

---

[y] A similar wooden coffin formed from the trunk of an oak, split in two for the purpose, both parts being of nearly equal capacity, and still retaining the bark upon them, was found a few years since in a tumulus at Gristhorpe, between Scarborough and Filey, and contained the skeleton of what was supposed to be an ancient Briton. With it were found a brass and flint spear-head and flint arrow-heads, a wicker basket, &c., the particulars of which were published in a pamphlet by Mr. William Williamson in 1834. It appears from a passage in the Earl of Ellesmere's very useful " Guide to Northern Archæology," that this discovery and a similar one at Biolderup form the subject of a paper in the Nordisk Tidskrift for Oldkyndighed.—T.

composed of several layers of coarse woollen stuff, sewn together, and also some locks of brown human hair, a sword with
a handle, and a dagger of bronze, a paalstab as they are
termed, a brooch, also of bronze, a horn comb, and a small
round wooden vessel with two handles at the sides, in which
was found something which had the appearance of ashes.

In the description of this discovery, which is quite peculiar
of its kind in this country, it is not mentioned that any remains of an unburnt corpse were observed, which appears singular, because the stem was so far hollowed out that the
corpse of a grown man could be placed in it. It is however possible, that in the construction of this barrow, a rule,
of which we have already given some examples, has been
followed, namely, that the weapons and trinkets have been
placed in the most distinguished part of the barrow, while the
vessel of clay, which contained the remains of the burnt corpse,
was merely placed in the heaped up earth.

The barrows of this period were placed, wherever it was
possible, on heights which commanded an extensive prospect
over the surrounding country, and from which in particular the
sea could be distinguished. The principal object of this
appears to have been to bestow on the mighty dead a tomb
so remarkable that it might constantly recall his memory to
those living near, while probably the fondness for reposing
after death in high and open places, may have been founded
more deeply in the character of the people. Such a desire
would seem of necessity to be called forth by a sea-faring life,
which developes a high degree of openness of character, since
the man who has constantly been tossed upon the sea and has
struggled with its dangers, would naturally cherish a dislike
to be buried in a corner of some shut up spot, where the
wind could scarcely ever sweep over his grave. For this
reason there are traces that the upper surface of several considerable heights, for instance Boobierg in Jutland, and Skam-
lingsbanken in Sleswig, were used as burial-places by those
who were too poor to construct barrows of their own. The

cinerary urns here are merely placed about a couple of feet deep in the earth, and without any other protection than a circle of small stones.

The barrows of the bronze-period occur in much greater numbers and extent, both in the islands, and in Jutland, Sleswig, and Holstein. Where the greatest number are found, the population was probably most numerous. Yet the multitude of barrows in single spots induces the idea of battles, after which the fallen were interred on the field. These barrows are met with both in the districts on the coast, which were those first inhabited, as well as in the interior of the country, which at a later period was gradually cleared of wood. It follows thence that they are not to be referred to any very brief period, but rather belong to a long series of years, in which various, and now unknown events, may have occasioned the immigration of allied races of people. As they also date from a period in which, particularly towards the close of it, a connection with other countries, and by this means the opportunity of learning and adopting their manners and customs, was opened, which could not of course be the case during the stone-period, it will as little surprise us that they occasionally differ in structure and arrangement, as that, without exception, they contain corpses unconsumed by fire. These are found in small narrow cists of stone, which are composed of thin flat squares of stone, covered with similar ones; but this mode of interment scarcely came into use till towards the close of the bronze-period. Many of these tombs have also been constructed after the more recent civilization, characteristic of the age of iron, had begun to produce its effect on the people; and from this we can easily perceive that the ancient usages were no longer so closely observed.

III. TOMBS OF THE IRON-PERIOD.

We may regard as a result of the circumstance that the iron-period can have commenced only at a comparatively recent date in Denmark, the fact that there exist but very few tombs which can with certainty be referred to it, while of those of the bronze-period there exists a very considerable number. Notwithstanding the circumstance that from this cause our knowledge of the Danish tombs of this period is extremely imperfect, it is still very evident, that between the tombs of the iron, and those of the bronze-period, some difference exists, although that difference is not so marked as that between the tombs of the stone and of the bronze-period. The external form and in some measure the internal structure of the tombs are in particular very similar, while they differ most with regard to the mode of interment, the tombs of the stone-period usually containing unburnt corpses, while those in the barrows of the bronze-period have, generally speaking, been burnt. It is true it was the custom in Sweden and Norway, in the iron-period, to consume the remains of the dead by fire, but of such a practice we find no vestiges, or at least very faint ones, in the tombs of Denmark belonging to the same period.

With reference to the mode of interment which prevailed in the North during the heathen period, the celebrated Icelandic historian Snorro Sturlesen, who wrote a chronicle of the Norwegian kings six hundred years ago[z], remarks that it was at first customary to burn the dead, and this period was termed the age of burning ; but at a later period, after the interment of Frej, at Upsala, without the burning of the corpse, many chiefs buried their relatives in barrows, and hence the age of interment took its origin. In Denmark Dan Mikillati (the Splendid or the Proud) was the first who was buried without being burnt. He caused a large barrow to be con-

---

[z] The Heimskringla, or Chronicle of the kings of Norway, of which an English translation in three volumes was published by Mr. Laing in 1844. The antiquarian reader will however be pleased with a German translation by Mohnike, (Stralsund, 1837,) who un-fortunately died shortly after the publication of the first volume. His notes and commentaries upon Snorro's work afford most interesting and valuable illustrations of the early history of the North.—T.

structed, and ordered that when he was dead he should be brought and interred there, in his royal pomp and armour, together with his horse and saddle and various other objects. With this occurrence the age of interment commenced in Denmark, yet the age of burning lasted long after among the Swedes and Norwegians. In Denmark therefore the age of burning corresponds with that of bronze, and the age of interment with that of iron. It must however be remembered, that tradition often refers a remarkable change in certain previously existing customs, to certain prominent personages, and so in this case the change in the mode of interment is ascribed in Sweden to Frej, and in Denmark to Dan. The historical foundation for the interment of Dan Mikillatti may probably be that in the age of interment the mode of burial may have been far more splendid and costly than in the so styled age of burning, of which fact the barrows themselves afford very remarkable proofs.

The greater part of the few barrows of the iron-period, which have hitherto been examined in Denmark, are distinguished by the circumstance that they contain not only the remains of the warrior, but also those of his horse[a]. Thus in a barrow near Hersom, in the Rindsharde, domain of Viborg, the skeleton of a man together with that of his horse, and with these an iron sword, a spear, a stirrup, a bridle with a chain bit, and a cross bar at the ends, were discovered. In the same manner in a barrow near Hadberg, in the Galtenharde, domain of Randers, portions of the skeleton of a man and a horse were observed; near them lay an iron axe, a pair of stirrups, and a bridle. In a very large tumulus on the field

[a] See on this subject a curious note in the appendix to Mr. Kemble's translation of Beowulf, descriptive of the obsequies of a Teutonic hero.

In an extract from the *Fornaldar Sögur*, edited by Rafn for the Antiquarian Society of Copenhagen, which relates the particulars of the funeral of Haralldr Hildita vn, is a very characteristic passage descriptive of the slaughter of the horse, and the placing the chariot and saddle in the mound, that the hero may take his choice between riding or driving to Valhalla.—T.

of Möllemosegaard, in the Sallingherred, domain of Svendborg, were found some years ago the skeletons of a man and a horse, and near them a number of iron objects, among which was a bridle which has been covered with thin plates of silver. In addition to this the barrow also contained several remarkable ornaments for harness, and a large metal vessel[b]. The Sagas

[b] In a paper by the Rev. E. W. Stillingfleet, in illustration of some Antiquities discovered in tumuli on the wolds of Yorkshire, published in the York volume of the Archæological Institute, will be found a remarkable account of the discoveries of two distinct skeletons of what Mr. Stillingfleet designates British charioteers, from which the following are extracts.

"In a cist almost circular, excavated to the depth of about a foot and a half in the chalky rock, and on a nearly smooth pavement, the skeleton of a British charioteer presented itself, surrounded by what in life formed the sources of his pride and delight, and no inconsiderable part of his possessions. The head of this charioteer was placed to the north, with an eastern inclination. He rested on his back, his arms crossed on his breast, and his thigh and leg bones, when bared, presented to the eye what may be termed a singular grained work : both the thigh and leg bones appearing to have been crossed in opposite directions. Very near to his head were found the heads of two wild boars. Inclining from the skeleton, on each side, had been placed a wheel : the iron tire and ornaments of the nave of the wheel only remaining. The tire of the wheel to the east of the body was found perfect in the ground ; but unfortunately it broke into several pieces on removal, owing to its corroded state. Small fragments of the original oak still adhered to the iron. In diameter these wheels had been a trifle more than two feet eleven inches ; the width of the iron tire about one inch five-eighths. The diameter of the ornaments of iron plated with copper, and varnished green, which had encircled the nave as a kind of rim, was very nearly six inches. The circumference of the wheel, on the western side, had been forced much out of its shape, evidently by pressure of the earth. Each of these wheels had originally rested on a horse, the bones of which were found under or adjoining to them : the head of each horse being not far from that of the charioteer on opposite sides. From the sizes of their leg bones these horses were of unequal height : but probably neither of them reached thirteen hands. Perhaps they may lawfully be regarded as progenitors of the Shetland, Welch, or forest breeds of our own day ; at any rate, they corroborate by the most certain of all evidence the historical record that the British horse was 'diminutive in his size, and swift in his motions.'" ** "On the western side of the British charioteer were found two very singular articles of the length of five inches ; round at one end, and curved at the other : of iron plated with green-varnished copper, which our workmen called linch-pins. Besides these (in different parts of the barrow, but all I think on the western side) were found two little rings, three quarters of an inch in diameter, and five buckles, semicircular, of various sizes, in some of which the tongue still remained. These buckles undoubtedly belonged to the harness, and their fellows may be seen in the Stanwick collection."

mention the circumstance, that the northern Vikings of ancient times were often buried in their ships, over which a barrow was erected; such a mode of interment however, as far as we are aware, has never yet been discovered in any Danish barrow, although it is not improbable that traces of it might be found. It is perfectly natural that the Viking should cherish the wish that his bones should repose in the ship which was his most valuable possession, and which had borne him to foreign lands, to booty and to fame.

In consequence of the increase of the wealth of the North, which was the result of the expeditions of the Vikings, the barrows were constructed on a larger scale than formerly. Among the most remarkable and most costly of the tombs of the iron-period, are those barrows which have sepulchral chambers of wood; one barrow in particular of this kind has been preserved, which, from its peculiar arrangement and the historical recollections associated with it, has no equal in the North. King Gorm the Old, who at the end of the ninth or the beginning of the tenth century, first united the

"On the same side, near the legs of the skeleton, were found two other appendages of the equipage of this British charioteer, in full length about ten inches. They are formed by two substantial rings, of the outer diameter

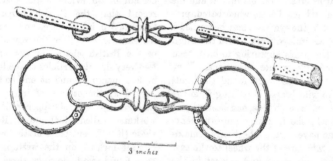

3 inches

of three inches and a quarter, joining on strong globular links, being tied together by another strong double link of two inches three quarters long. Like the rest of the articles found, they are of iron, plated with copper, coated with green; and the large rings have a pretty chain-pattern running round them. These articles would generally be pronounced to be the bits of bridles: objects similar to these have often been discovered, and may be seen both in the Stanwick and Polden Hill collections."—T.

numerous small kingdoms of Denmark into one connected
whole, married Thyre the daughter of a petty king of Jütland
or Holstein.   This queen, who is celebrated in legend and in
song, distinguished herself even in early youth by a love
for her country, and an ability and integrity, which secured
her a lasting memorial in the hearts of the Danes.   It is
narrated that Gorm while he was wooing her had dreams,
which Thyre interpreted, and by this means averted a dread-
ful famine from Denmark.   Out of gratitude the Danes named
her Danebod, or the " Ornament of Denmark," a name which
she well deserved, since she subsequently erected in Sleswig
the celebrated wall or Danewall, (Danevirke,) which served to
protect Denmark against hostile incursions.

On her decease, Thyre Danebod was interred after the old
northern custom in a vast barrow, which is still to be seen
at Jellinge, in Jütland, close to the north side of the church.
On the barrow a reservoir was gradually formed, to which
miraculous powers were attributed, and in the course of years
the sick and the lame made pilgrimages to the spot.   On the
water becoming dry, it was desirable to cleanse out the funnel-
shaped cavity which formed the reservoir, and thus an opportunity was given for examining the tumulus.   The searchers
first came to a number of small stones, and next to a
remarkable burial chamber formed of wood.   It was about
twenty-two feet long, four and a half high, and covered with
beams of oak.   The walls, which had been covered with
woollen cloth, were formed of oak planks, behind which was
a bed of clay firmly trodden down, on which the beams of the
ceiling rested.   The flooring consisted of oak boards, which
were very carefully placed close to each other without being
actually joined together.   The ceiling had also been provided
with oak planks.   In this, which was doubtless at that time
regarded as a very splendid mausoleum, no remains of bones
were discovered, but a chest was found in the form of a round
coffer, which was almost consumed by decay.   Near it lay the
figure of a bird, formed of thin plates of gold, and the silver

cup already described, (page 72,) which was covered inside
with a thin plating of gold. Besides this were found merely
another figure of a bird, and some other trifles of less importance, such as the remains of metal plating, painted pieces
of wood, &c. The contents of this remarkable barrow were
comparatively unimportant, but it had been opened before.
It was plainly discernible that four of the beams of the ceiling
had been cut through at some previous time, and that an
entrance to the tomb must have been effected in this way,
probably by the well-known openers of barrows in the middle
ages. The discovery of a short wax candle, placed on one of
the beams of the ceiling which had been cut through, still
more confirms this supposition.

Opposite to the barrow of Thyre, on the other side of the
church at Jelling, is seen a similar elevation, in which her
consort King Gorm is interred, which however has not yet
been examined. These tumuli are the largest and most considerable in the whole country, their height is about seventy-
five feet, and their circumference at the base above five hundred and fifty feet. Such mounds are extremely rare in the
North. Usually, the barrows are only from twelve to twenty-
two feet, the latter size being very uncommon.

It is worthy of notice that at the same period, when large
elevations were thus piled over deceased persons of distinction,
bodies of wealthy persons were deposited in the natural sand-
banks. In several places in this country, for instance in the
parish of Herfölge, at Himlingöie, in the domain of Vallö, at
Sanderumgaard, and at Aarslev in Fühnen, there have been discovered in sand-banks where no artificial barrows were perceptible, unburnt bodies, trinkets of gold and glass, together with a
buckle with a Runic inscription, mosaic birds, in short, objects
which with reference both to the shape and the material, are
undoubtedly to be referred to the latest period of paganism.
The circumstance that several corpses are here usually found
interred, leads to the conjecture that towards the close of the
heathen period there were general places of interment, which

form the transition to the custom which became prevalent in the Christian era of interring the dead in church-yards[c].

IV. Tombs in other countries,
(particularly in Sweden and Norway.)

In order that the Danish memorials may appear in their true light and connection, it will be of importance to enquire in what regions of other countries similar monuments of antiquity have been observed. Without such a general examination it would scarcely be possible to derive satisfactory historical conclusions from the enquiry.

We first turn then towards the South. Stone chambers, or cromlechs, or low barrows, encircled with stones, which completely accord with the cromlechs of our stone-period, occur in Pomerania, Brandenburg, Mecklenburg, Hanover, in fact in the whole of the north of Germany, in England, Ireland, Holland, (particularly in the northern part,) and in the west and south of France. Their contents are everywhere the same. Where they have not previously been opened there occur skeletons with objects of stone and amber; or one meets with stone implements and fragments of vessels of clay, just as in Denmark. Thus in France cromlechs of the stone-period, which contained skeletons and implements of flint, have been found, not only on the western coast, but also singly in the middle of the country, even in the southern part itself, in the neighbourhood of the Pyrenees and of Marseilles. They occur also in Portugal and in Spain, while, as far as is known, they never have been discovered in the interior parts of Europe, in the south of Germany, Italy, Austria, or the east of Europe. They are very distinct from the tombs of the pagan era of those countries, both in their structure and their simple funereal contents.

[c] Such large burial-grounds without tumuli, of the Anglo-Saxon period, are traceable in this country in the Isle of Thanet, Northamptonshire, and other localities.—T.

The limits of the tumuli or barrows of the bronze-period cannot be so well defined, since these, as regards their form and general arrangement, have much similarity with most of the tumuli of Germany and other European countries of that period, in which the practice of burning the dead generally prevailed. Barrows which contain bronze objects with spiral ornaments, like ours in Denmark, do not occur farther south than in Mecklenburg, and possibly in Hanover; and on the contrary, barrows, with bronze articles of somewhat different character, occur in most countries of the south and west of Europe, both on the coasts and in the interior parts.

The barrows in the three northern kingdoms differ very much from each other.   The cromlechs and giants' chambers of the stone-period, which occur generally in Denmark, meet us only in the south-western part of the present Sweden, particularly in the old Danish country of Skaane in West Gothland, in Holland, and Bahuslehn; but they are not found at all in the north-east and north of Sweden, *nor in the whole of Norway*.   The barrows, cairns, and stone circles of those districts have a totally different character; the large and peculiar cromlechs disappear both from the exterior and interior of the barrows.   Above all, however, it is to be observed, that the bodies have not been deposited unburnt, except at a much later period; in the more ancient, burnt remains are always met with.   Although this mode of interment was prevalent in Denmark during the age of bronze, yet the barrows in Norway and Sweden which lie north and east of the limits of the cromlechs of the stone-period, have scarcely any resemblance to the barrows of Denmark of the age of bronze; for these have about the same limited extent in the peninsula of Scandinavia, as the cromlechs and giants' chambers of the stone-period.   A short description of the monuments of Sweden and Norway will illustrate the difference of the graves in the three kingdoms of the North.

As soon as we penetrate from the completely Danish districts of the south-west of Sweden, with a new aspect of nature, new memorials of antiquity also meet us. Instead of wide, extended, and fertile plains, we see only rocks, which are either altogether unproductive, or grown over with scanty trees, and with them innumerable masses of stones which have rolled down. This abundance of stone, and consequent deficiency of loose earth, cannot have been without its effect on the external arrangement of the barrows. Barrows composed of mounds of earth are henceforth considerably lower than in Denmark, while those which chiefly consist of stone are the most prevalent. An object almost unknown among us is the cairn (steenrör), as it is called, which frequently lies on the highest rocks, and by which are indicated barrows which are destitute of any covering of earth, and are composed of a heap of stones piled together, on the floor of which an oval stone cist is usually found. They are occasionally of very considerable size, for instance more than twenty feet in height and fifty paces in diameter. The other barrows, which are somewhat more numerous, and are partly mixed with earth, are considerably smaller, since they are constructed of very small stones heaped together, and hence they but seldom rise more than from three to five feet above the surrounding surface. Great variety is observable in their form. Usually they are either circular or oval, and enclosed by a circle of stones, in which the single stones are close to each other; occasionally they are quadrangular, and often with a larger stone at each corner; and again they occur of a triangular shape. The last mentioned, which in general have sides much bent inwards, are often adorned with an erect and somewhat lofty stone in the centre, where the grave itself is placed, and with a similar one at each of the three ends. Yet there are also circular and quadrangular enclosures of stone which do not surround heaps of stone mixed with earth, but merely a level surface. These have been named places of justice, (Tingsteder,) or of sacrifice and worship, (Offersteder,) or of contest, (Kampkredse.) That they also, at least in general, are graves, is evident from the circumstance that they are met with in great numbers, and contain urns of clay, with burnt bones, ashes, and other antiquities. The most remarkable places of interment in Sweden are un-questionably the ship barrows (Skibssœtninger), as they are named.   By this term is understood an oblong enclosure of

stones running to a point at the ends, which is filled with a heap of small stones mixed with earth, while occasionally the space enclosed is quite level.   At each end is usually seen an upright stone, by which doubtless the stem and stern of a ship are indicated.   The resemblance to a ship is still more obvious from the circumstance that there exist similar enclo-sures of stone, with a tall stone in the middle, in imitation of a mast, and with several rows of small stones which go across the enclosure, and represent banks of oars.   They lie chiefly in the neighbourhood of the sea, for instance in Gothland and Oeland, but in particular in Bleking, where they are met with in several places in considerable numbers, associated with round, square, and triangular graves ; at the place called Lis-terby Aas alone are seen about a hundred, although many have perished in the course of time.   They differ considerably as to size, occurring from eight to sixty paces long, and two to fifteen paces broad : in the larger ones the terminal stones are from twelve to sixteen feet in length.   In general they are to be considered as burial-places of the Vikings[d] ; in single

[d] It appears from Mr. Worsaae's large and more important work, en-titled "*Zur Alterthumskunde des Nor-dens*," 4to. Leipsig, 1847, p. 17, that there have been found in some of these ship barrows tolerably large iron nails, such as are used in the construction of small ships or boats ; so as almost to convert the supposition that such bar-rows have been the burial-places of

instances they may have been erected in memory of some engagement at sea.

The tall narrow standing stones termed "Bautastene," or memorial stones, were unquestionably, as the name indicates, memorials; they are usually from nine to twenty feet long, and stand in the middle or at the side of the barrow. At Stenehede in Bahuslehn are seen nine entire bauta-stones, and three which have been split in two, in a  row fifty paces long, between oval and round barrows. But still more remarkable is the field of battle situated not far from the above at Gresby, in the parish of Tamune, where, in a short space, about a hundred and thirty very low barrows, partly round, partly oval, and surrounded with stones, occur, of which about fifty appear to have been adorned with standing stones, from seven to fifteen feet in length. There are about forty of these stones remaining, but only sixteen stand erect[e].

Vikings into something like a certainty; and to confirm the assertion of the Sagas, that the bodies of these heroes were first burnt in their ships— that the ashes were then covered with earth, and the grave encircled with stones in the form of a ship.—T.

[e] The subjoined woodcut, reduced from a lithographic print in the larger work by Mr. Worsaae, mentioned in the preceding note, represents a view of a number of bauta-stones now existing at Hiortehammar.—T.

With the exception of the extensive king's barrows near
the church at Old Upsala in Sweden, which in size may be
compared to the barrows of Gorm and Thyre, at Jelling, in
Denmark, and thus may justly be reckoned among the most
remarkable monuments of the North, which are formed of
earth, the barrows of Sweden, as has already been mentioned,
are strikingly low.   Hence they include only in single instances any large structures of stone or wood.   In this particular they differ from the barrows of Norway, which, if they
consist of earth, are, taken as a whole, more extensive, both
as regards their internal and external arrangements.   They
not unfrequently cover several wooden structures, in which
many and valuable antiquities are placed.   This is particularly the case with the Norwegian cairns.   In general, however, the resemblance between the tombs of Norway and
Sweden is very obvious.   The same low round quadrangles,
triangles, and ship-like barrows, surrounded with stones, as
well as the standing stones, are found in these two neighbouring kingdoms.   Among the monuments of antiquity
were formerly reckoned a peculiar kind of large stones, which
are so placed on the edges of rocks that they may be made to
shake merely by the strength of the arm, without losing their
equilibrium ; hence they are usually called Rocking-stones,
(Rokkestene.)   Several such have been discovered at Bornholm, and in great abundance in Norway and some parts of
Sweden. They were formerly considered to have been heathen
altars or oracles.   It is now, however, believed that they
are merely rolled stones, which, from various natural causes,
have been loosened from the rocks, and have acquired such a
position that they can be shaken without falling down.

The barrows of Sweden and Norway have not only a peculiar external form, but as regards their contents they are
essentially different from the Danish barrows.   The latter
usually contain antiquities of the stone and bronze period,
which is never the case with those of Sweden and Norway,
since they, almost without exception, contain antiquities of the

iron-period, such as weapons and implements of iron, shell-shaped brooches with open-work, interlacing ornaments and filigree-work, and beads of glass and mosaic. Besides, the corpses placed in them are burnt, while those of the Danish graves of the iron-period are almost always interred in an unburnt state. Traces of such a mode of interment in barrows occur but rarely in the Norwegian barrows, and more rarely still in those of Sweden, and then they are always of the period of the transition from paganism to Christianity. By this circumstance the statement of Suorro is confirmed, that the age of burning lasted longer in Sweden and Norway than in Denmark. There is another fact which must not be overlooked, that in Denmark the age of burning corresponds with the age of bronze, but in Sweden and Norway with that of iron.

On account of the agreement in date, it must be mentioned that graves are seen in Iceland, (which country was first peopled by immigrating Norwegians at the end of the ninth century,) which completely resemble the places of interment common in Norway and Sweden, which are low and enclosed with stones, and which lie in many districts associated with ship-like barrows, and with triangular and quadrangular enclosures of stone. From the foregoing enquiries it will be perceived that similar enclosures of stone and low barrows of earth, together with the long and narrow stones erected over them, are scarcely to be observed in Denmark. It is true there is a report that in the domain of Apenrade, in the neighbourhood of the sea, several of these ship-like enclosures, the Dannebrog ships, (Dannebrogskibene,) as they were called, have been found. There are likewise some stone enclosures at Hiarnoe, which appear to bear some resemblance to these ship-formed enclosures, but they are unique of their kind, and as their origin moreover is very doubtful, they naturally cannot be considered to outweigh the obviously according testimony of all other barrows. The result of the comparison between the monuments of Denmark and those

of the rest of the North is therefore as follows.   In Denmark
and the south-west portion of the present Sweden there are
numerous cromlechs of the stone-period and barrows of the
bronze-period, and but a few tombs from that of iron, and
those only from the most recent period.   On the other hand,
in the rest of Sweden and in Norway there are neither cromlechs from the stone-period nor barrows of the bronze-period,
but in their stead a number of peculiar barrows and stone
enclosures, which are different from those of Denmark, and
which belong both to the earliest and latest period of the age
of iron[f].

The tumuli, therefore, fully accord with the antiquities,
since they shew that the stone and bronze periods do not
apply to Norway and Sweden as they do to the ancient
Danish districts, and that the later period of the iron age
comprises all three kingdoms; that Norway and Sweden,
however, were immediately its home, whence it perhaps extended itself at a later period over Denmark.   This fact
clearly indicates that in very ancient times Denmark was
more fully peopled than the other nations of the North.

It is worth observing, that the same mode of interment
which prevailed in Denmark in the later part of the iron-
period, viz., that of burying the dead *unburnt* in large burying
places, without raising tumuli or barrows over the graves, also
prevailed both in the north and south of Germany, in Mecklenburg, Bavaria, Baden, in Switzerland, Alsace, France, and
in England.   In all those countries this mode of interment
undoubtedly was used immediately before the introduction of
Christianity.   In some of these burying places there have been
found Christian crosses or ornaments, and also Christian
inscriptions.

Since we are thus enabled by a knowledge of the arrangement, the age and the relations of which the barrows of Den-

----

[f] Cf. Worsaae, Blekingske Mindes-   Zur Alterthumskunde des Nordens.
morker for Hedenold, translated in   Leipzig. 1847. 4to.

mark bear to the memorials of other countries, to distinguish the tombs of different ages, we are by this means enabled to correct many an erroneous tradition which has, from time to time, crept into history. Some explanatory instances of this sort may not be wholly without interest.

In the battle, so celebrated in early history, which took place at the Braawalla-heide in Sweden, between the Danish king, Harald Hildeland, and the Swedish king, Sigurd Ring, Harald Hildeland fell in the conflict. His corpse, so the ancient records relate, was placed on a funeral pile and burned, and his ashes brought to a tumulus raised at Leire, which tradition still points out. It is somewhat injured, but consisted in ancient times of an oblong elevation of earth, of about seventy to eighty feet in length, and twenty-four feet in breadth; on each of the long sides stood ten erect stones, the four corner stones being somewhat larger than the rest. On the north side, was a small barrow of earth, at the foot of which was the grave itself. This was formed of three large and two small stones placed in a quadrangle; the square between was filled with small flat stones. On the large stones once rested a large roofing stone, which was destroyed a hundred years ago. The whole appearance of the tomb will be rendered more plain from the accompanying illustration.

From this figure it will be evident, beyond all doubt, that this is merely a common cromlech of the stone-period; in fact, wedges of flint have been found in the earth, which has been excavated from the chamber; and thus it is obviously impossible that it can have been erected to Harald Hildeland, who, according to the narratives of the ancient Sagas, must have lived at a much later period. We might cite a number of similar unfounded tales of tombs, in which certain well-known kings, for instance Humble and Hjarne, are said to have been interred; but we will point out only the most remarkable and celebrated of the whole, namely, that of King Frode Fredegode, (or the Lover of Peace,) whose corpse was borne for three years about the country before it was buried. It was finally interred in the long extensive barrow at Værebro Mölle, in the neighbourhood of Frederickssund in Seeland. The tradition is of such antiquity that the celebrated historian Saxo Grammaticus, six hundred years ago, recorded it from an ancient ballad. Frode's barrow, as it is called, is a long elevation, which appears to have been formed by human hands, and at a distant period was surrounded with large stones, several of which were remaining a few years ago. At one end of the barrow is a semicircular cavity, from which extends a depression of the soil to the side of the hill. In this hollow lie several large stones, the remains of the destroyed funereal chambers. About a hundred years ago, Bishop Rönnor caused the chambers to be examined, but nothing was found in them, except a heap of human bones, such as usually occur in graves of the stone-period, among which this Frode's barrow must be included. If Frode Fredegode is to be regarded as an historical personage, it is probable that he may be interred at Værebro, but one cannot help doubting whether he reposes in the tomb to which tradition has assigned his name, for in his time bodies were certainly no longer placed in cromlechs. On the whole the country near Værebro and Leire is particularly rich in cromlechs of the stone-period, and no doubt for this reason, that those districts which were favourable for hunting and fishing had considerable attractions for the aboriginal inhabitants. That "the great place of sacrifice" of the kings of Leire, near Snoldeler, in the parish of Vor Frue, (Our Lady,) at Roeskilde, which consists of a barrow surrounded with stones, with three chambers, is also nothing more than a cromlech of the stone-period, may safely be assumed from what has been already stated.

The importance of critical illustrations of this nature, acquired by means of barrows, is not confined to the circumstance that certain unfounded traditions, which have partly been collected in later times, are by this means destroyed and banished from history. We learn beside, which is of equal importance, that such traditions can only be received with the greatest caution, even when they relate to particular spots and barrows, and when the reference dates some hundred years back, unless peculiar circumstances confirm the date and authority.

V. RUNIC STONES.

Antiquarian remains and barrows would convey much more trustworthy information of the past if they were in all cases furnished with inscriptions. From the languages in which such inscriptions were composed, we should then be able to form conclusions as to the descent and connection of the earliest inhabitants of the North; since, it is sufficiently clear that men who belong to the same stock, speak languages which are, at all events, allied to each other. But unfortunately inscriptions of ancient date are extremely rare. In the stone-period, writing, with the exception perhaps of single hieroglyphic signs and representations, appears to have been completely unknown. Of the bronze-period no distinct traces of inscriptions appear to have been discovered; and it is only in that of iron, that inscriptions occur which are inscribed in the so termed Runes, or Runic letters. The usual alphabet, which consists of sixteen characters, is as follows:

ᚠ. ᚢ. ᚦ. ᚮ. ᚱ. ᚴ. ᚼ. ᚾ. ᛁ. ᛅ. ᛋ. ᛏ. ᛒ. ᛚ. ᛘ. ᛦ.　　ᛦ.

F. U. Th.O. R. K̄.Ḡ. H. N. I. A. S. T̄.D̄. B. L. M. Y.　　R.
　⌣　　　　　　　　　　　　　　　　　　　　　　(Oe) (at the end.)
(soft D.)

There are, however, deviations from the above, and several varieties of the characters themselves; beside which there are other various kinds of foreign Runes still more different, such for instance as the Anglo-Saxon. Inscriptions of this kind, probably on account of some unknown peculiarities in their arrangement, are, generally speaking, very difficult to interpret.

In ancient times the Runes were scratched on metal, as in the case of trinkets and ornaments, or were carved on wood, particularly on staves of wood and on bark, or were engraved on stone. As wood, bark, and in some degree metal, are in the course of time consumed in the earth, those inscriptions are best preserved which are met with on the large stones, which, from the Runes, are called Runic stones.

These are usually tomb-stones, which have been erected over the graves of deceased persons of distinction. The Runic stones belong partly to the pagan, and partly to the early Christian period. As an unquestionably pagan Runic stone may be mentioned that at Glavendorp in Fuhnen, discovered at the beginning of the present century. The inscription which is divided into three parts is inscribed on its three sides, and may be rendered into English, as follows : 1. "Raynhilde placed this stone to Ale Solvegolde, a man well deserving of honour." 2. "The sons of Ale erected this barrow to their father, and his wife to her husband, but Sote inscribed these Runes to his lord. May Thor bless these Runes." 3. "Accursed be he who moves this stone, or takes it to another place." It is deserving of particular attention, that Thor, their deity, is here particularly appealed to. In general the inscription on the stone merely records by whom, and for whom, it was erected, with the addition of various circumstances. These inscriptions are therefore generally uniform, yet they afford valuable and interesting details for history, particularly with reference to domestic relations. They seldom refer to foreign, great, or important events.

Among the most remarkable stones in Denmark, in this respect, are the two monumental stones at Jellinge, over Thyre Danebod, and Gorm, and the stone at Söndervissing. Of the Jellinge stones, which are both to be seen before the

church door, the smallest was erected by Gorm to Thyre. It
is of granite, five feet high, and three feet broad, and somewhat flat. On the two broad sides is the inscription.

FRONT.

REVERSE.

That on the front is, according to the characters, "Gumer
kunugr garði kubl ðosi aft ðurvi runu;" and that on the
back, "sina Danmarkarbut." "King Gorm constructed this
barrow to his wife Thyre Danmarksbod." That Gorm is
here mentioned as having erected the barrow to his wife is
peculiarly striking, since all authors agree that Thyre sur-
vived Gorm. In case, therefore, we do not assume that the

barrow was erected and the stone engraved while Thyre was still living, which is by no means without example, or authority, we must, of necessity, conceive that authors have left us very imperfect details of these events, and that Thyre actually died before Gorm.

The large stone at Jellinge was erected to the memory both of Gorm and of Thyre, by their son King Harald Blaatand. It is eleven feet high, and has, on its three sides, an inscription which runs thus: "King Harald caused this barrow to be made to his father Gorm, and his mother Thyre; the same Harald who acquired all Denmark, and Norway, and Christianity as well," (that is, caused his people to be baptized.) On the third side of the stone is inscribed a figure of Christ, which is recognisable by the circumstance that in the nimbus round the head the points of a cross are to be seen. By this emblem our Saviour was always distinguished from the Saints in the early representations. The Runic stone consequently affords, by means of the inscription and the figure of Christ, a valid contemporaneous proof of the introduction of Christianity into Denmark. It is not only a memorial of Gorm and Thyre, but is equally a monument of the triumph of Christianity over paganism; and hence it may justly be styled the most remarkable monument in Denmark, if not, in the whole North.

The Runic stone at Söndevissing, in Tyrstingherred, in the district of Scanderborg, which was only discovered a few years ago, appears to have been erected about the same time as the great stone at Jellinge. The inscription is "Tuva lot görva kubl, Mistivis dotir uft muður sina, kuna Haralds kins guða Gurmssunar." That is, with the addition and explanation of certain words, "Tuva caused this barrow to be constructed; she was a daughter of Mistivi; she made it to her mother, and was the wife of Harald the Good, son of Gorm." By Harald, the son of Gorm, we cannot but suppose that Harald Blaatand is intended; and, if it were confirmed that mention is here actually made of him, this inscription acquaints us with a fact which was hitherto unknown, namely, that his wife was named Tuva. The whole of the history of that period is so defective that we cannot wonder at the name of a queen not being mentioned by historians. The Runic stone further adds that Tuva was a daughter of Mistivi, a statement which, in this case, is of double interest, since we know from other sources that there existed, at that period, a Wendish prince named Mistivi, (possibly the same as the Mistivi of the Runic stone,) who in the year 986 destroyed Hamburgh. Harald must in such case have stood in such relation to the Wends, as in a political point of view, could not be without importance with reference to Denmark.

Although instances are most rare in which Runic stones afford such important historical information, yet viewed collectively they deserve peculiar attention, even those which seem to have very unimportant inscriptions [g]. Since, in fact, inscriptions are the oldest relics of language which we possess, the Runic stones must be considered as the oldest monuments both of the extent, and the construction of the language of antiquity. With reference to the decision of the often contested question as to the diffusion of the Danish language towards the South, in ancient times, it is of no mean importance, that at the south-east end of the ancient wall of Kograven in Sleswig, which lies somewhat south of the Dane wall or Danevirke, and is unquestionably very ancient, Runic stones have been discovered with inscriptions in the ancient

[g] The most useful works on the subject of Runes, to which our English antiquaries, with the exception of Mr. Kemble, have hitherto paid but comparatively little attention, are W. Grimm *Ueber Deutsche Runen ;* J. G. Liljegren's *Run-Lara,* 8vo., Stockholm, 1832 ; the same author's *Run-Urkunder,* published at Stockholm in the following year, which contains all the existing Runic inscriptions ; and W. W. Dieterich's *Runen Worterbuch.* The English reader will find ample information upon the subject of Anglo-Saxon Runes, in Mr. Kemble's learned dissertation in the Archæologia, (vol. xxviii. p. 327, et seq.,) and his subsequent communications, entitled, "Further Notes on the Runic Cross at Lancaster," (vol. xxix. p. 76, et seq.,) and his "Additional Observations on the Runic Obelisk at Ruthwell, the poem of the Dream of the Holy Road, and a Runic Copper Dish found at Chertsey," (vol. xxx. p. 31, et seq.)—T.

Danish tongue. Since it is further known from history that, in ancient times, one language was spoken throughout all Scandinavia, a circumstance which is confirmed by the fact that the inscriptions on the Runic stones in the three northern kingdoms, are written in one and the same language, with merely casual variations caused by peculiar circumstances, it can scarcely be doubted, that a thorough investigation into the collective Runic memorials of the North will afford important assistance towards a knowledge of the Danish tongue in its most ancient form; and thus contribute to its improvement in future times. The number of Runic stones in Denmark is not very considerable; and in order to obtain the desired result from their investigation, it will not only be necessary to keep a watchful eye over the preservation of those already known to exist, but attention must, in like manner, be directed to the discovery of others. There are undoubtedly numerous Runic stones still existing, either buried in the earth, or standing in places where the inscriptions are not seen; at all events, such stones have constantly been discovered from time to time, several of which have been very remarkable. It is peculiarly desirable when blocks of stone are to be split, that care should first be taken to ascertain whether any inscriptions exist on their sides, and should such prove to be the case, the stones ought to be preserved for more complete investigation.

Before any correct idea was formed of the value of Runic stones many remarkable monuments had been entirely destroyed. At the present day, however, when the love of our native tongue strongly prevails, it is to be hoped that the most ancient memorials of the Danish language will not be destroyed from indifference, or for the sake of a trivial gain.

THIRD DIVISION.

I. Importance of the Monuments of Antiquity for History.

From what has been already stated, it is clear that we are enabled, by means of the antiquities and barrows, to form much clearer ideas, as to the peopling and civilization of Denmark, in primeval times, than could be derived from the uncertain and imperfect written memorials of those times. This fact will best appear from a general review of the advantages which the investigation of these monuments of antiquity has afforded to history.

In the time of the aborigines, the stone-period as it is called, when Denmark was a rude and thickly wooded country, it was inhabited by a people who, for the most part, diffused themselves along the sea-coast. They occupied a low rank in civilization. The use of metals was unknown to them, and hence all their implements were made of stone, of bone, or of wood. With such tools the inhabitants could make no great progress in agriculture; on the contrary, hunting and fishing formed their chief sources of subsistence. For catching fish in rivers, and in the sea, they used hooks, harpoons, and lances of flint, and they possessed boats formed of stems of trees which had been hollowed out for the purpose[h]. When hunting, they were armed not only with bows and arrows, but also with lances and hunting knives, the more easily to slay the large animals, whose skins served them for garments. Their dwell-

[h] While these sheets have been passing through the press, several remarkable specimens of these ancient canoes have been discovered in this country. One found in the neighbourhood of Southampton is described in the Literary Gazette of the 2nd of July; another, measuring about twenty-two feet in length, was taken out of the Tay at Sleepless Island in the early part of the present year; and a third has been discovered at Glasgow, fifteen feet below the old Cross of that town.—T.

ings were formed most probably of stone, wood, and earth, for they even buried their dead with much care in Cromlechs, which were formed of large stones, smooth on the inner side. By the side of the dead were laid their hunting and fishing implements, of bone and stone. Similar Cromlechs, with similar contents, are to be seen on the south coast of the Baltic, and on the north-west and west coasts of Europe, in England and Ireland, but have not been found either in the interior of Europe, in Norway, or in the northern parts of Sweden.

In the next period, or during the age of bronze, a greater degree of cultivation was introduced into the country, and by this means all previous relations were completely changed. The natives were now in possession of two metals, bronze, (a composition of copper and tin,) and gold. They possessed woven cloth, and handsomely wrought trinkets, weapons, shields, helmets, and wind instruments, which were adorned with peculiar embellishments, particularly with the so-called spiral ornaments. Bronze tools gradually supplanted the implements of stone, which however continued for a long time to be used by the poorer classes; and hunting and fishing gave way to agriculture, which was then commencing. The forests in the interior of the country were cleared by degrees, in proportion as agriculture was more widely extended, and the population increased. Intercourse with other countries was opened, partly by means of warlike expeditions, partly by commerce: navigation acquired importance, and ships were built of a larger and better description, than the simple vessels formed of hollow trees. At this period it was customary to burn the bodies of the dead, and to deposit the bones which remained in cinerary urns, in small stone cists, or under heaps of stones in large mounds of earth. Sometimes the bodies were also interred unburnt in stone cists, which are however always totally different, both in size and form, from the Cromlechs of the stone-period. Barrows containing implements of bronze are found in great numbers over nearly the whole of Europe, except in Norway and Sweden, where they are extremely rare.

At length, and as appears about the eighth century, the third age, or the iron-period, was completely established. With it came into use in Denmark two metals, hitherto unknown and unused, iron and silver, but, of course, it took a long time before they came into general use. All cutting tools and weapons were now made of iron, instead of bronze, and were moreover completely altered in regard to form. The trinkets and ornaments were altered not only in form, but also in the material of which they were composed; being no longer made of bronze, (copper and tin,) but of brass, (copper and zinc.) On the whole, an entirely new taste prevailed in this period, which was a natural consequence of the connection of the North with other countries, which had attained to a higher civilization. By this means many foreign objects were brought thither, which were afterwards imitated by native smiths. To the east and south-east, the people of the North had connections in the way of trade with the eastern portion of the Roman empire, the countries of the Caspian sea, and the coasts of the Baltic.

A very great influence also on the developement of civilization in the North was produced by the frequent hostile expeditions of its inhabitants to the west, to England and France, from which countries were introduced the germs of many useful improvements. Agriculture made no particular progress in Denmark at this warlike period, since the people were constantly engaged, either in predatory expeditions into other countries, or in repelling the attacks of strangers at home. It was of course perfectly natural that the taste for agriculture and similar peaceful employments should be lost at a period, when expeditions by sea brought as much fame as booty. But, that no small degree of civilization must have existed at that time in Scandinavia appears from the splendid ornaments and weapons, and the powerful vessels, which the Northmen then possessed. The modes of interment were now somewhat different from those of the bronze-period. The corpses were chiefly buried unburnt, either in large barrows or mostly in natural beds of sand, and with them many beautiful and costly ornaments. The Viking was buried in his ship; and the hero was often accompanied in the grave by his weapons, and his favourite horse. The remains belonging to this period are incomparably more numerous in Norway and Sweden, than in Denmark.

This division of the ancient times in Denmark into three periods is solely and entirely founded on the accordant testimony of antiquities and barrows, for the ancient traditions do not mention that there ever was a time here, when, for want of iron, weapons and edged-tools were made of bronze. On this account, many maintain that no importance, or credibility, can be attached to this division into three eras, since the objects supposed to belong to such three periods may have proceeded from the same period, but from different classes of persons. Thus, they assume that the bronze objects, which are distinguished by their beauty of workmanship, may have been used by the rich; while the iron objects belonged to those less wealthy, and those of stone to the poor. This supposition is scarcely founded on probability, much less on a perfect acquaintance with the remains of antiquity.

It is quite true that tools and weapons of stone and bronze, and perhaps also of stone, bronze, and iron have, as has already been remarked, been in use at the same time, *in periods of transition*, when bronze or iron was scarce in the country, and consequently very expensive; yet it is nevertheless no less true, that there were three distinct periods, in which the use of stone, bronze, and iron severally prevailed, in a most characteristic manner.

For if it be granted that bronze objects belonged only to the rich, how is it to be imagined that there were no, or rather exceedingly few, rich people in the northern parts of Sweden, and in the whole of Norway, where, it is well known, that, comparatively speaking, bronze objects belong to the rarest finds. Moreover it is scarcely probable that the rich would have used the inferior metal, bronze, for tools and weapons, while those less wealthy possessed the superior, iron. Beside, we meet with fewer trinkets, and in particular far fewer large gold ornaments, with the bronze ornaments than with those of iron; with the bronze objects, silver trinkets, and Cufic, or East Roman, coins are never found. Again, if we assume that iron objects were the property of the rich, and those of bronze of persons less wealthy, in short, of the poor, this supposition is alike improbable, since in this case there can scarcely have been poor men in all Norway and Sweden! With reference to the stone objects, or those assigned to the very poor, it is proper to observe that they are usually found in the large Cromlechs and Giants' chambers. But the Cromlechs and Giants' chambers are much larger and more splendid monuments than the barrows which contain the objects of bronze; one would therefore be driven to the conclusion that the rich were buried in a mere mound of earth, thrown up over an unimportant heap of stones, while the poor, on the other hand, were interred in chambers of stone, which from their size and their careful style of building, often excite the admiration of the present age. This, of course, is wholly incredible. Again, if the objects of bronze and of iron belonged to one and the same period, it would be highly probable that they would be wrought in the same fashion, or that, even when the metal was different, their forms and ornaments would exhibit some resemblance, however slight. But the bronze antiquities betray in their form, ornaments, and workmanship in general, a totally different character from that which is exhibited on objects of iron. Finally, if the different kinds of antiquities were really cotemporaneous, one must at any rate expect that our barrows, which must be regarded as cotemporaneous also, would possess as their chief characteristic, and particularly with reference to their modes of interment, a certain similarity to each other, which might easily be recognised. But we know that the large Cromlechs and Giants' chambers contain objects of stone and *unburnt* corpses; that those barrows which contain bronze objects with *burnt* corpses have a totally different arrangement ; and that barrows and other tombs with iron objects are essentially *different* from the other barrows. Since it cannot be supposed that, in ancient times, so strict a separation of the three classes, the rich, the middle class, and the poor, can have prevailed, that each class had its peculiar mode of interment, together with weapons, tools, and trinkets, which both in form and material were totally distinct from those of the other classes, it must therefore be regarded as an undoubted fact, that the often-named division of antiquities and barrows into three ages, is founded not on probability alone, but on positive facts, and on a much firmer basis, than might have been expected when the question relates to a period which lies beyond the limits of satisfactory historical details. We therefore have no hesitation in proceeding to the further enquiry, whether it was one race only which in ancient times developed itself in a gradual manner, or whether several races have from time to time penetrated into the country, and occasioned these changes in its civilization.

Experience has shewn us that modes of interment, and all circumstances appertaining to them, are most prized and preserved by nations in an inferior degree of civilization, and are only abandoned by them, when they have been subdued by foreigners more powerful than themselves, or when they have ceased to be an independent people. In the stone-period, and in that of bronze, the funeral ceremonies and barrows were completely different; and we are therefore justified in concluding that the race who inhabited Denmark in the bronze-period was different from that, which during that of stone, laid the foundation for peopling the country. This is clearly shewn by the antiquities, since there exists no gradual transition from the simple implements and weapons of stone, to the beautifully wrought tools and arms of bronze. On the other hand, it is not decided that the people of the iron-period must have been a third race, which had immigrated at a later date than that which inhabited the country during the bronze-period ; for though the antiquities and barrows of these two periods are by no means of the same kind, yet the difference is neither so striking, nor so prominent, as to enable us to found on it the supposition of two totally different races of mankind. A greater developement of civilization, and in particular a more lively intercourse with other nations, might easily, during a more advanced period of paganism, have called forth a remarkable alteration both in the prevailing taste, and in the mode of interment. The most that we can say, at present, is that Denmark, during the iron-period may possibly, by small immigrations from the neighbouring countries, have received new constituent parts of its population. Since, therefore, it appears from the evidence of its monuments that Denmark was inhabited, in ancient times, by two different races, let us seek whether any sufficient explanation respecting the families of mankind, to which those races must be referred, is contained in the most ancient historical records, or whether we must be satisfied with the information which these monuments themselves afford us.

§ 1. THE STONE-PERIOD.

History mentions the Fins and Celts as being among some of the first inhabitants of Europe. The Fins, or Laplanders, as they are called at the present day, now live far towards the north ; at a former period, they reached farther to the south, at least over the greatest part of Sweden and Norway, and, in the opinion of many, even over other countries, from which they were driven eventually by the intrusion of later immigrants. The vestiges and remains of the Celts are likewise confined within very narrow limits, in England, Scotland, and Ireland ; though, in remote ages, they were the most powerful and the most widely diffused nation in the west of Europe. From this circumstance, historians have hitherto assumed that the Fins and Celts, in ancient times, bordered on each other in the North, and that they here formed the first population of the northern part of Europe.

Hence it would naturally be believed that the inhabitants of Denmark, during the stone-period, were either Fins or Celts. Of the Fins we are told by Tacitus, who lived in the first century after the birth of Christ, that they were extremely rude and poor. They possessed neither weapons, horses, nor houses. They fed on roots, clothed themselves in the skins of beasts, and spread their couch on the bare earth. Their sole resource was their arrows, to which, from the want of iron, they affixed points of bone. Even their children had no refuge from storm and shower; they were merely covered with branches of trees twined in each other. This description of the mode of life of the Fins, agrees in every essential particular, with that contained in all other ancient records. As the inhabitants of Denmark, during the stone-period, were not acquainted with the use of any metal, but lived by hunting and fishing, the opinion has often been expressed that those ancient inhabitants of Denmark were Fins, and hence that all the Cromlechs, Giants' chambers, and antiquities of stone, were memorials of this aboriginal Finnish population. As a farther proof, appeal is made to the circumstance that stone implements, of the same kind, are often found in all the three northern kingdoms of Scandinavia, consequently that the whole of Scandinavia has been inhabited by the same race, and what people could it be but the Fins, who have inhabited Sweden, and Norway, from the earliest times.

Such a conclusion is, however, by no means to be relied on. It is quite evident that the circumstance of implements of stone, which bear great similarity to each other, having been discovered in Sweden, Denmark, and Norway, by no means justifies us in concluding that such implements were used by the same people. For since implements of stone, which are perfectly similar, occur in Japan, in America, in the South Sea islands, and elsewhere, we must, in case we adopt that conclusion, necessarily assume that branches of the same race, which, in ancient times, inhabited the northern parts of Europe, must also have reached as far as those countries. Yet these antiquities can only shew that the races, who used the same objects of stone, stood in something like the same degree of civilization; but if more precise information of historical interest is desired, then the form and contents of the tombs, or of the still existing memorials, must necessarily be taken into consideration. It is, however, an acknowledged fact, that the peculiar Cromlechs and Giants' chambers of the stone-period, are never found either in the north of Sweden or Norway, (where, however, remains of the Fins, up to the historic period, have been preserved;) nor even in those countries which are still inhabited by the Finnish races. The associations are here totally different. The inhabitants, therefore, during the stone-period cannot have been Fins, who were gradually driven towards the North by other nations; for it is utterly incredible that during a retrograde movement, which they undertook in order to preserve their independence, they should on a sudden change their ancient modes of interment, and the customs which they had inherited from their ancestors. Beside they repaired to spots which abounded in granite rocks and loose blocks of stone, and where, consequently, it would have been easier for them to construct Cromlechs and Giants' chambers, than in Denmark.

The Fins, in fact, appear to have left no memorials of their abode in the southern districts of Scandinavia; they were in the earliest times, as now, little other than a mere nomadic race who had no regular or fixed abodes, and who might therefore easily disappear from a country without leaving any traces of their existence in it, as soon as it was no longer capable of supplying them with the means of subsistence. The inhabitants of Denmark during the stone-period must, doubtless, have attained a higher degree of civilization than the ancient Fins. They must, at all events, have possessed fixed dwellings, otherwise they would scarcely have constructed those remarkable Cromlechs and Giants' cham-

bers of stone, which remain as lasting monuments of the
energy and skill of the builders. It has, however, been supposed by some that the Fins, at the time they lived in Denmark, had fixed abodes, and that they first commenced their
nomadic life, when they were driven by a newly invading and
more powerful people, from the fertile southern part of Scandinavia, to the more northern parts, to the wild woody mountains
of Sweden and Norway, which would account for the want of
Cromlechs, in those countries. But it is evident that a people,
who leave a country for the sake of defending their independence and nationality, neither give up their usual way of earn-
ing their livelihood, nor their old peculiar national customs;
except when obliged to emigrate to a country where they
are compelled to alter their mode of living because they cannot find the same means for subsistence, or when frequent
attacks of their enemies will not allow them to settle quietly,
and continue the observance of their religious customs, &c.
Nothing of that kind could have happened to the Fins in
going from the south, to the north of Scandinavia. Both
Norway and Sweden have plenty of coasts, woods, and rivers,
full of game and fish, which would afford to a fishing and
hunting people, a most excellent opportunity for fixed abodes;
perhaps even more so than Denmark. It must also be remarked, that it is said to have been the new invading people, in the bronze-period, who expelled the Fins from Denmark. But in Norway this new people do not seem to have
settled, as there remain scarcely any monuments at all of
them. In Norway, therefore, the Fins, after having been
expelled from Denmark, could have settled quietly, and continued hunting and fishing, and burying their dead in Cromlechs and Giants' graves, after the manner of their forefathers,
without being troubled by their enemies in Denmark.

It would nevertheless be a strong argument in favour of
the Finnish origin of the Cromlechs, if, as some authors contend, the skulls and skeletons which are found in these graves,
had exactly the same characteristic type, as the heads and cra-

nia of the present Laps. But hitherto so few skulls from Cromlechs have been preserved, that it is scarcely possible to found any argument upon them; though it seems that the skulls, which have as yet been excavated, so far from being of the same type, are so different, that a physiologist declared some of them to be of *Caucasian* origin. It is not sufficient to attribute this difference to an effect of the difference of climate, and the altered mode of living adopted by the Fins, when they went from the south to the north of Scandinavia, because this is only an hypothesis, which, as has already been shewn, is far from tenable. It is therefore not improbable that, thousands of years ago, a nomadic race connected with the Fins, whose existence it is, at this moment, impossible either entirely to deny, or to establish satisfactorily, may have wandered about Denmark; while this much is certain, *that the inhabitants of Denmark during the stone-period cannot have been the Fins, whose descendants are the present inhabitants of Lapland.*

From a conviction of this fact, other writers have argued that the Fins have formed the basis of the earliest population in Sweden and Norway only, but that the Celts were the most ancient inhabitants of Denmark. This view, at the first glance, seems a highly probable one, since it is known that the Cromlechs and antiquities of the stone-period occur on the coasts of the whole of the west of Europe, as well as in countries, which were certainly inhabited by the Celts from the earliest times. But in these countries there also exist Barrows, which exhibit a striking similarity to the Danish Barrows of the bronze-period. We might therefore with equal right maintain that such Barrows were constructed by the Celts, since they occur in countries which are known to have been inhabited at a very early period by that people. It is impossible to form any conclusions, in this respect, from the Barrows. The Celts, however, according to all historical records, were early distinguished by a certain degree of civilization; they possessed weapons and ornaments of metal, there were regular towns in their countries, and it has even been ascertained that, in certain districts, they coined money. Since it was their custom mostly to burn the bodies of their dead, and inter them in Barrows, it is clear that the Celts must have been a totally different people from the inhabitants in the stone-period, who interred their corpses unburnt in Cromlechs, and used mere simple implements of stone and bone. It may certainly well be imagined that the Celts originally existed in a lower state of civilization, and that by degrees they acquired a knowledge of the use of metals, and thereby the opportunity for greater improvement. It must here, however, be remembered that the Celts, at the period when they are first mentioned in history, spread themselves from Italy through the west of Europe (or Gaul), to England (Britain.) Thus they possessed about the same countries in which the Cromlechs occur. At that time, however, they had been driven by the German races towards the west. In previous times they had undoubtedly occupied a much greater extent of the present country of Germany, particularly its middle and southern parts, where the names of localities, mountains, and rivers, are very frequently of Celtic origin; in which regions, however, the characteristic Cromlechs with unburnt bodies, instruments of flint, and ornaments of amber, have not as yet been found. Had Cromlechs of this nature been the most ancient Celtic graves, we should certainly have expected to have found them in the countries first inhabited by the Celts. But, what is more, in the west of Europe there appears not to have been any transition from the Cromlech to the Barrow; they are totally different.

According to all probability we must, on the contrary, assume that the people who inhabited Denmark during the stone-period, and who, as we learn from the remaining memorials of ancient times, diffused themselves over the coasts of the north of Germany, and the west of Europe, as well as in England and Ireland, were not of Celtic origin; but that on the contrary they belonged to an older and still unknown race, who, in the course of time, have disappeared before the immigration of more powerful nations, without leaving behind them any memorials, except the Cromlechs of stone in which they deposited their dead, and the implements which, by the nature of their materials, were protected from decay. History has scarcely preserved to us the memory of all the nations who have from the beginning inhabited Europe; it is therefore a vain error to assume that certain races must incontestably be the most ancient, because they are the first which are mentioned in the few and uncertain written records, which we possess.

Meantime there is a method by which we may probably, in the course of time, be enabled to ascertain to what peculiar race of men the first inhabitants of Denmark belonged. By an examination and comparison of the different people, and the different regions of the earth, it has been found that the several races of men present remarkable varieties in their physical conformation, and that these varieties are most observable in the shape of the skull. Several men of science have, as already mentioned, commenced examining and describing the skulls and skeletons found in the Cromlechs, and Giants' chambers of the stone-period. It has, by this means, been proved that the people by whom these were erected were, with reference to corporeal structure, neither above nor below the middle size, but to what race of men they may most suitably be referred has not yet been fully ascertained. Formerly but little attention was paid to these skulls, for which reason comparatively very few, and those in an imperfect state, have been preserved in our collections. When greater interest shall have been awakened for the antiquities of our country, and consequently a larger number of skeletons shall have been procured, we may reasonably hope to acquire, by means of comparison, certain historical results which may possibly lead to other and more important discoveries, as to the descent of the aborigines.

Although history affords no explanation as to the race

here mentioned, yet we may possibly, by means of probable conjectures, arrive at something like a knowledge of the place they occupy in the history of the people of the north, and west of Europe. All facts, for instance, seem to shew that Europe was not peopled at once, by a race of mankind who bore in themselves the germ of all future progress, but that this race has gradually received the addition of others, who continually supplanted the former, and laid the foundation for a more advanced civilization. The first people who inhabited the north of Europe were without doubt nomadic races, of whom the Laplanders, or as they were formerly called, the Fins, are the remains. They had no settled habitations, but wandered from place to place, and lived on vegetables, roots, hunting and fishing. After them came another race, who evidently advanced a step farther, since they did not follow this unsettled wandering life, but possessed regular and fixed habitations. This people diffused themselves along those coasts which afforded them fitting opportunities for hunting and fishing; while voyages by sea and agriculture also appear to have commenced among them. This race however seems not to have penetrated the interior parts of Europe, which were at that time full of immense woods and bogs; they wanted metal for felling trees and so opening the interior of the country, for which purpose their simple implements of stone were insufficient. They followed only the open coasts, and the shores of the rivers, or large lakes. To this period belong the Cromlechs, the Giants' chambers, and the antiquities of stone, and bone, exhumed from them.

Then again came races who possessed metals, and some degree of civilization, and they, being able to cut down the woods, occupied not only those regions of the coast which had been previously inhabited, but also the interior of the country. But they likewise appear, in the first instance, to have followed the course of the rivers, and, from them, in the progress of time, to have spread themselves more and more over the neighbouring countries. It was by them that agriculture, and its consequent civilization, were first regularly established. Among these races there were in the west the above-named Celts. The inhabitants of Denmark, and the west of Europe, in the stone-period, are therefore to be designated as forming the transition between the most ancient nomadic races, and the more recent agricultural and civilized nameless tribe.

It has been said, that it would be rendering little service to historical knowledge, to introduce such a nameless, and hitherto unknown, people into the history of Europe. A mere name is certainly of scarcely any importance. The principal thing is, that we have, by means of this people, discovered the way in which Europe was inhabited in the earliest time, a point upon which historical records do not furnish us with any account. We have seen quite a new step of civilization, and that is the first and important discovery made through the study of the primeval antiquities of Europe. It seems highly probable that this aboriginal people have not disappeared at once, but that they have been subdued by a new invading race, and by them, after the manner of other conquerors, reduced to slavery. The slaves in the North in pagan times, are described in the oldest traditions, as being entirely different in appearance from the other classes.

It will at once be seen that the stone-period must be of extraordinary antiquity. If the Celts possessed settled abodes in the west of Europe, more than two thousand years ago, how much more ancient must be the population which preceded the arrival of the Celts. A great number of years must pass away before a people, like the Celts, could spread themselves over the west of Europe, and render the land productive; it is therefore no exaggeration if we attribute to the stone-period an antiquity of, at least, three thousand years. There are also geological reasons for believing that the bronze-period must have prevailed in Denmark, five or six hundred years before the birth of Christ.

§ 2. THE BRONZE-PERIOD.

The inhabitants of Denmark, during the bronze-period, were the people who first brought with them a peculiar degree of civilization. To them were owing the introduction of metals, the progress of agriculture and of navigation, not to mention that the previously uninhabited districts in the interior of the country were, by them, cleared of wood and rendered productive. This people stood therefore in the same degree of civilization as the Celts, and exercised as important an influence over the civilization of the north, as the Celts over that of the west of Europe. Is it then probable that the people of the bronze-period must themselves be regarded as a Celtic race?

The ancient written accounts of the early times of the North afford no sufficient authority for assuming that the Celts ever lived in the North; but they contain certain indications which, it has been thought, may possibly refer to something of the kind. For instance, the earliest Scandinavian traditions and songs mention that those races who had last migrated into the North, lived on friendly terms with a people named the Alfs, who, at an earlier period, lived at Alfheim, in the south of Norway, and in the north of Jutland. Since the Alfs, from what is related of them, must have possessed some civilization, and have been acquainted with agriculture, several historians have recognised in them the remains of Celtic tribes, who had formerly possessed larger portions of Denmark, from which they had been gradually ejected by other races. It is likewise said, that the peninsula of Jutland was inhabited by the Cimbri, who were probably of Celtic origin, and hence that it acquired the name of the Cimbric peninsula. These Cimbri, in such case, were to be regarded as the remains of the ancient and universally diffused Celtic population. By means of such naturally unfounded conclusions, it might be rendered apparently probable, that the inhabitants of the country during the bronze-period were Celts, particularly as antiquities of bronze similar to the Danish ones, have frequently been found in all the countries which were formerly, and are still, inhabited by Celtic tribes. It has been said too, that the bronze weapons, implements, and ornaments were of Celtic origin only, because the Teutonic tribes had no miners, and did not understand how to prepare the bronze metal, or how to work it afterwards.

It is certainly very curious that the many weapons, implements, and ornaments of bronze, which have been discovered in Greece, Italy, Germany, France, England, and Scandinavia, have in many respects considerable resemblance to each other. The swords are all short, two-edged, and with small handles, which have been fixed with nails to the blade; the Celts have about the same form, and have been fixed nearly in the same manner into the handle. The forms of the hatchets, knives, arm and neck rings, &c., are also very much alike. They have all been cast in moulds, and the metal is of the same composition, nine-tenths copper and one-tenth tin. From this there would be farther reason to suppose that they all originated with one people.

But a careful examination and comparison of the antiquities themselves from these various countries will nevertheless shew that in different countries the antiquities of bronze are also somewhat different. First the *patterns* or ornaments are not at all the same in all countries. In the North, in Denmark, and Mecklenburg, the *spiral* ornaments are, as already shewn, the most prevailing; but farther south, and west, *ring* ornaments and lines, which sometimes form triangular figures, are alone to be seen. Of the *forms* too the details are different. In Denmark, the swords of bronze have more often peculiar bronze handles, richly ornamented, than in England; in Italy again the forms of the swords are a little different both from the English, and the Danish ones. The Celts in Italy, Switzerland, and Greece, are much flatter, and more ornamented, than the Celts in the north of Europe. The lance-heads in the British islands are distinctly different from the Danish, which unlike the

British, never have loops at the side of the shaft-hole. There is no doubt but that, in time, we shall be able to point out quite distinctly the limits for the different forms and patterns.

From what has here been said, we may conclude that the antiquities of bronze do not belong exclusively to one people, in the north, west, or south of Europe ; which is further confirmed by the discovery in nearly every country of Europe, of the moulds in which the various weapons and ornaments of bronze have been cast; a fact which shews beyond a doubt that such bronze objects were manufactured in those countries, and not imported. The only thing which was imported being of course the metal, which by trade and barter was spread; in different ways, over the whole of Europe.

It is also well known that the classical authors do not mention copper, or bronze, as having been used instead of iron exclusively by the Celtic tribes. On the contrary, they mostly mention iron weapons among the Celts, but speak of bronze weapons as used by people who were not Celts. It is stated by Homer, Hesiod, and other authors, that the Greeks in the most ancient time, before they had knowledge of iron, used bronze, which was also the case with the Romans. Herodotus, speaking of the Massagets, a Scythian or Finnic people, living to the east of the Caspian sea, says, that they had neither iron nor silver, which were not to be found in their country, but that they had plenty of copper and gold : on which account all their lance-heads, arrow-heads, and war-axes, were of copper, and their caps and belts ornamented with gold. The same author speaks also of other Scythians, who used weapons of copper; to which must be added, that the Egyptian, and Siberian tombs and barrows, often contain tools and weapons of bronze, and copper.

From these evidences it follows that the antiquities belonging to the bronze-period which are found in the different countries of Europe, can neither be attributed exclusively to the Celts, nor to the Greeks, Romans, Phœnicians, Sclavonians, nor to the Teutonic tribes. They do not belong exclusively to any one people, but have been used by the most different nations, at the same stage of civilization ; and there is no historical evidence strong enough to prove that the Teutonic people were in that respect an exception. The forms and patterns of the various weapons, implements, and ornaments are so much alike, because such forms and patterns are the most natural, and the most simple. As we saw in the stone-period, how people at the lowest stage of civilization, by a sort of instinct, made their stone implements in the same shape, so we see now in the first traces of a higher civilization, that they exhibit in the mode of working objects of bronze, a similar general resemblance. But it is quite clear that the civilization in the bronze-period was only preparatory. It principally existed as long as the people spread themselves over the countries, cutting down woods, and beginning to cultivate the soil ; in short, so long as they did not appear actively on the stage of history. At the moment they did so appear, we find them in possession of iron, and of the higher civilization which went along with it. Already in the time of Homer the Greeks had iron, although it was very scarce and expensive ; the Romans seem to have had, and used iron, before the kings were expelled. It was partly an effect of Greek and Roman influence, that the use of iron was known at a comparatively early period in the northern parts of Italy, in South Germany, and Gallia, the inhabitants of which countries were thereby enabled to contend so gallantly with the Romans. Polybius mentions however, that the Gauls, who about two hundred years before Christ, fought against the Romans in the north of Italy, were obliged in their battles to straighten their swords by putting their feet upon them, because they bent when exposed to a heavy blow ; a fact which shews that the Gauls did not then possess steel. The invention of making the iron hard is attributed to the Celts of Noricum ; in the time of Augustus, the Noric swords were famous in Rome.

But if the people in the neighbourhood of Rome, and influenced by Roman civilization, at the commencement of the

Christian era, generally possessed weapons of iron, it does not follow that the people in the North had also, at so early a time, plenty of that metal. Cæsar says distinctly that, in Britain, iron was only to be found at the coasts, and that in such small quantities that the inhabitants used imported bronze, ("*ære utuntur importato.*") It must also be remembered, that he speaks of their using iron rings, as money. A century after Christ, the Britons seem to have got a great deal more iron, but the Germans had still so little of it, that they very rarely had swords, or large lance-heads, of that metal. It was when the Romans got colonies in Hungary, Germany, Gaul, and Britain, or about from the third century of the Christian era, that their civilization first got some influence in the northern part of Germany, and in Scandinavia, where however it evidently had a hard struggle with the old civilization.

This view is strongly supported by the antiquities and tombs in the different countries. The many Gaulish and British coins which, there is no doubt, were originally imitations of the coins of Philip, and Alexander the Great of Macedon, shew a very early Greek influence, which most likely spread itself over Gaul and Britain, from the Greek colony at Marseilles. But it is particularly important that *all the antiquities* which hitherto have been found in the large burying-places *of the iron-period* in Switzerland, Bavaria, Baden, France, England, and the North, exhibit traces more, or less, of Roman influence. The common pattern is an interlaced and arabesque ornament, (the snake ornament as it has been called above, p. 72,) which is not at all like any of the old ornaments in the bronze period, but bears a close resemblance to Roman patterns, and mosaic pavements, and many other objects of Roman art. In imitating the Roman patterns there have been added fantastic figures, and heads of animals, and men. In some of the large burying-places, as near Basle in Switzerland, the tombs were built of broken Roman tomb-stones; and in other tombs of the same period, both in Germany and England, there have frequently been found Roman coins, belonging to the first centuries after Christ, but none older. The objects found in those tombs, exhibit a remarkable general resemblance, not only in pattern, but also in form; this however affords no proof, that they were manufactured by one people, and by them spread over Europe, because the details differ in different countries. On the contrary in the iron-period we see again a common step of civilization for the European people; we find the first traces of the new civilization, which rose upon the ruins of the Roman civilization, but which necessarily commenced with imitations of the preceding one. But, at the same time, the tombs shew that this imitation commenced later in the north, and particularly in Scandinavia, than in the south, and west of Europe. In the Scandinavian tombs of the iron-period there have never been found, as in those of southern and western Europe, Roman coins dating from the first centuries after Christ; for the Roman coins, which have been discovered in the North, have been turned up in fields, sand-banks, &c., but never in tombs. Celtic coins have never been discovered in Scandinavia. The oldest coins which have been found in the North, in connection with antiquities of the iron-period, are Byzantine coins, or more commonly imitations of Byzantine coins, the bracteates of gold, which are for the most part imitated from coins of the fourth, fifth, and sixth centuries. The imitations of the coins are then of course of a still later date. Thus, the tombs of the iron-period in the south shew an earlier influence from Rome, but the northern tombs, of the same period, shew a much later influence from Byzantium. It is therefore not only easy to understand why the remains of the old civilization in the bronze-period are so rare in the south of Europe, and so numerous in the north, particularly in Ireland and Denmark, where the Romans never were, but it will also now be much easier to explain the monuments of the bronze and iron-period, in Scandinavia.

We have seen, not only that the antiquities of the iron-period are comparatively speaking very scarce in Denmark; but also that the cairns, stone-circles, and standing stones, which are characteristic of the iron-period, and which are to be found in such considerable numbers in Norway and Sweden, at once stop at the old borders of Denmark, where they are completely unknown, and where again the remains of the bronze-period, which are nearly unknown in Norway, and the northern part of Sweden, are exceedingly common. This seems to afford a strong argument that the civilization of the iron-period, which can first be traced with any certainty in Sweden and Norway, as late as the fourth and fifth centuries, must have been completely introduced into Denmark at a still later date. It is in that respect worth observing, that the tombs of this period in Norway, and Sweden, consist of barrows of the old fashion, in which the bodies were interred after having been *burnt;* but, that the tombs in Denmark belonging to the same period form large burying-grounds, in which the bodies were buried *unburnt.* This custom does seem not to have prevailed before, in the transition from paganism to Christianity; on which account, there have been found in these burying-places, both in Switzerland and in the south of Germany, Christian inscriptions and Christian emblems.

The remains of the iron-period in Denmark are scarcely sufficient to fill up a couple of centuries, before the first commencement of Christianity, (826); and we cannot therefore carry the complete introduction of the civilization of the iron-period into Denmark farther back, than to the sixth and seventh centuries.

About the year 500, it seems to have been introduced into Mecklenburg, as the Slavonic people took possession of the land, which was left by the Saxon people, who went over to England. But the civilization was sooner and more easily introduced into Mecklenburg by the new invading people than into Denmark; where evidently, the same people who lived there in the bronze-period continued to keep possession of the country, and maintain the old civilization; if they had been expelled by a new invading people, who first settled in Sweden and Norway, we should of course expect to find the same monuments of the iron-period in Denmark, as in Norway and Sweden, which as we have seen, is not at all the case. It is however, natural, that those people who inhabited Denmark, at the time of the invasions into Norway and Sweden, should be mixed with some fresh elements.

Under these circumstances, it cannot possibly be imagined that the inhabitants of Denmark in the bronze-period should have been Celts. If they also, as late as the sixth and seventh centuries, had mixed with the Scandinavian people, which is in the highest degree improbable, we should have reason to expect that the present Danish language would exhibit a considerable number of Celtic words and expressions, not to be found either in the Swedish, or in the Norwegian language; but this is very far from being the case. The oldest Runic inscriptions in Denmark, are as pure Scandinavian, as any other in the North. In the very place, in Norway, where Celts are supposed to have lived, tombs and antiquities of the bronze-period have never, as yet, been discovered. In fact, there does not exist any historical record of Celtic inhabitants in the North. The Roman authors say, certainly, that the *Cimbri* lived on the peninsula of Jutland. But the same authors speak of them as a Germanic people; and it must be remarked, too, that geographical knowledge was at that time exceedingly limited, so that accounts which refer to the northern peninsula of Holland, have sometimes been transferred to the peninsula of Jutland. The question here is not, how far a single, or small Celtic tribe, may have lived for a short time, during the bronze-period, on the peninsula of Jütland; but what people it was, who, during that period, was spread over the whole of the present Denmark, and the southern part of Sweden, and who have left behind them such a quantity of monuments.

Already, from the first centuries of the Christian era, the

Roman authors mention Gothic inhabitants of Scandinavia, which is farther confirmed by accounts in some of the oldest Icelandic Sagas, and chronicles of the North. It is there said, that Denmark, in the earliest time, was called *Eygotland* (the island of the Goths) and *Reiðgotland*, (the continent of the Goths,) or, by one name, *Gotland*. In the fifth century the Goths (Jütes) went over to England from Jutland, which country was still, in the ninth century, called by the Anglo-Saxons *Gotland*. "From Svea and Götaland the kingdom of Sweden has been formed in pagan times," says the old Swedish law-book. As therefore the remains of the bronze-period necessarily extend to the sixth and seventh centuries, there can be very little doubt, that the inhabitants of Denmark, in the bronze-period, were a *Gothic* tribe. It has however been said, that they were a Gotho-Germanic, and not a Gotho-Scandinavian race; and that they were quite subdued or expelled from Sweden and Denmark, by the Scandinavian people. But against this we have not only, as already shewn, the testimony of the monuments, but also the testimony of the history of Scandinavia. A general review of the iron-period will further prove, that this Gothic tribe must necessarily have been the first Scandinavian people, who settled in the North.

§ 3. The Iron-period.

The numerous remains belonging to the iron-period in Norway and Sweden must, without all doubt, be ascribed to the same people as the present Swedes, and Norwegians, (*Svear og Nordmænd;*) who, according to all tradition, came from the East, and who on their arrival in the northern parts of Scandinavia, either completely subdued the nomadic Finnic tribes living there, or drove them to the most northern part of Europe, where remnants of them exist to this day. Already, in the first century of the Christian era, Tacitus mentions the "Sviones" (*Svear?*) as having settlements in the North, on the borders of the Ocean. But if it is not to be supposed that the Sviones were the Goths, who in the bronze-period seem to have lived along the eastern and north-eastern coast of Sweden, and around the Mœlar lake, it is clear that there must have been later invasions. Both the oldest traditions and the monuments point to that. The whole civilization of the iron-period, which appears so suddenly in Sweden and Norway, that it must have come with a newly invading people, is evidently built upon the Roman civilization; the many Byzantine coins from the fifth and sixth centuries, which are found in the North, besides the imitations of them, the gold bracteates, the constant intercourse which, from that time, existed between the North and Byzantium, where the Northmen so frequently served as life-guards of the emperors, all seem, in a remarkable manner, to confirm the statement, preserved by the renowned Icelandic historian, Suorro Sturleson, that Odin and his followers, at the time of the Roman invasions of the countries of the Black sea, first left their settlement there, and went to the north-eastern part of Sweden, to the country around the Mœlar lake. It is quite natural that then, about a couple of centuries after Christ, new tribes should have entered Scandinavia, as it was at the time of the great "migration of people" (Germ. *Völkerwanderung*, Dan. *Folkevandring*), when nearly all the other countries of Europe were filled by new inhabitants.

The Svear, or as tradition says, Odin and his followers, came probably before the Norwegians. They appear to have passed from Russia, through Finland, over the Aoland islands, to the shores of the Mœlar lake, when they made their principal settlement in Upland, which was afterwards also called Mannheim, or the home of the men, or the people, and where the chief temple, or principal place of worship was, (at Upsala). From Upland, they peopled the neighbouring counties, which, from their situation with reference to Upland, were called Södermanland, Westmanland, &c., and which, together with Upland, were called Svithiod. The Norwegians, who came after the Svear, or Swedes, were now obliged to pro-

ceed still farther north and to cross over the Kjölen mountains, into Norway. From Halogaland far north, they went
down to Tröndelagen, around Drontheim, from whence they
spread themselves both along the coasts, and over the Dovre
mountains, over the interior, and southern parts of Norway.

About the year 400, or 500, Scandinavia was thus peopled
by Norwegians, Swedes, and Goths, who were divided into
Göths in Götaland, and Goths in Denmark. It is said that
the Swedes and Norwegians now expelled the Göths and
Goths, and took possession of their countries. But the
Swedes were separated from the Göths in Götaland, by wild
mountains and the immense forests Kolmorden and Tiveden,
from which Svithiod was called the land north of the wood
(Nordenskovs), and Götaland, the land south of the wood
(Söndenskovs); this made it, of course, very difficult for the
Swedes to attack the Göths. The Göths were first, in a later
period, about the eighth or ninth century, under the Swedish
kings, but that they were neither expelled, nor completely subdued, appears from the circumstance, that in the middle ages,
they still retained their own peculiar laws and customs, and
regarded themselves altogether as a distinct people. Until
nearly the fifteenth century, the Göths continued to contend
with the Swedes, respecting their share in the election of the
sovereign, &c.; and to this day, a difference both of dialect
and customs, serves to indicate that the Svear and Göths were
two nearly related, but, at the same time, two perfectly distinct people. The dialect, however, by no means shews that
the Göths spoke a German language; the dialects of Götaland,
as well as those of Denmark, were originally as pure Scandinavian, as the Swedish and Norwegian dialects. In the middle ages, only, they were perhaps more intermixed with German than the Swedish and Norwegian, because they had more
intercourse with Germany. It will easily be seen, that as
the Swedes could not expel the Göths, who were their neigh-
bours, the Swedes and Norwegians could still less expel the
Goths in Denmark, whó lived south of the Göths. This per-

fectly agrees with the existing monuments, and there is therefore little, or no doubt, that the Goths and Göths, the inhabitants of Southern Scandinavia in the bronze-period, were the
first Scandinavian tribes who settled in the North, and who,
of course, settled in the southern parts, as they were both the
most fertile, and the easiest to cultivate. The Goths and
Göths are thus to be regarded, as the real ancestors of the
present inhabitants of Denmark, and of the southern part of
Sweden; they afterwards became a good deal mixed with
the Swedes, and Norwegians.

The knowledge of iron, and the higher civilization, which
the Swedes and Norwegians brought to the South, and which
enabled them both to cut down the immense woods, make
roads over the mountains, cultivate the soil, and build large
vessels, was, by degrees, through intercourse, marriage, and
immigrations, spread over Götaland and Denmark. In
Götaland, the use of iron had probably completely superseded the use of bronze, for weapons and implements, as
early as the sixth century, as there were then in Götaland
frequent attacks both from Norway and Sweden, and as
Götaland, not long after, became connected with Sweden.
In Denmark it took of course more time; but from the fifth
or sixth century, the civilization of the iron-period had been
completely introduced into Mecklenberg, by the Slavonic
tribes; into England, by the Anglo-Saxons; into Norway,
and Sweden, by the Norwegians, and the Svear. It is probable that both bronze and iron were in use together in Denmark during one or two centuries, until about the year 700,
when the use of iron completely superseded that of bronze,
for implements, and weapons. At that time, they still, in Norway and Sweden, *burned* the bodies of their dead, and buried
them in barrows; but in Denmark, the custom was to bury
the bodies unburnt in large burying-places, which shews an influence from the west and south of Europe, where a similar
custom prevailed.

At this period, the mode of life in the North underwent a

great change. The Northmen were now so powerful that they made large settlements in the West, in England, Scotland, Ireland, France, &c. ; and in the East, in Russia ; which made Scandinavia, during several centuries, the central-point for an extensive commerce between the East, and the northern parts of Europe. Both by Viking expeditions, and by commerce, a higher civilization was brought from the West to the North. The many emigrations from Scandinavia weakened the power of the numerous small kingdoms ; and when Christianity was introduced into the North, independent conquering kings formed three larger kingdoms, of which Denmark contained the flat, and fertile, portions ; Norway the remote mountainous ; and Sweden the transition parts. It was now, that the three principal Scandinavian tribes, the Norwegians, Swedes, and the Danish Goths, got each their king.

We have thus seen how the antiquities and barrows serve to prove, that the flat fertile Denmark must have been peopled earlier, than the northern parts of Sweden and Norway, which were full of immense forests and mountains. The monuments shew the peopling of Scandinavia in a natural point of view ; which view finds confirmation, and that in a remarkable degree, rather than contradiction, in the most ancient and trustworthy of our historical records. Meantime, it is obvious, that most points of the present review of our subject can only receive their due explanation from future researches ; for science is as yet too young to furnish us, at once, with all the explanations which we require.

It has therefore been the peculiar object of the present work, merely to collect and compare the results obtained by science, up to the present moment, with the information afforded by history, in order to prove, to how great a degree, the antiquities and barrows have already afforded, and doubtless will continue to afford, important and indispensable information, not only to the ancient history of the North ; but, at the same time, to that of all Europe. With regard to the value of the information already acquired by these investigations into the monuments of antiquity, opinions will, of course, be divided; but, on the following point, all will certainly be of one opinion, namely, that a complete comparison of the antiquarian relics of different countries, with reference to the first peopling of Europe, and the most ancient history of the human race, will yield information, of the extent and importance of which, we are, at present, unable to form any adequate idea.

II. Importance of the Monuments of Antiquity as regards Nationality.

The age preceding the Christian era, on the consideration of which we have here dwelt for some time, forms a peculiar and very remarkable portion of the history of Denmark. We find our forefathers, it is true, devoted to a cruel and savage heathenism, but we cannot refuse them our admiration. Their love for freedom and for home, their truth and their bravery, which were the terror of the mightiest states in Europe, afford proofs of a nobleness of soul, and an energy, which are worthy of imitation at the present day. And, since it is certain, that the perusal of our glorious ancient traditions will powerfully contribute to excite the feeling for our independence of character, so, is it also certain, that antiquities and barrows, inasmuch as they explain these traditions, have also a deep importance for us, as national memorials. By their means, antiquity stands, as it were, revealed before our eyes. We see our forefathers penetrating, for the first time, into Denmark; and armed with sharp weapons subduing the uncivilized people who then dwelt here; we see them diffuse the knowledge of metals, of agriculture, and a higher degree of general civilization. We hold in our hands the swords, with which they made the Danish name respected and feared; we can even shew the trinkets and ornaments, which they brought home as booty, from their expeditions to foreign lands. The remains of antiquity thus bind us more firmly to our native land; hills and vales, fields and meadows, become connected with us, in a more intimate degree; for by the barrows, which rise on their surface, and the antiquities, which they have preserved for centuries in their bosom, they constantly recal to our recollection, that our forefathers lived in this country, from time immemorial, a free and independent people, and so call on us to defend our territories with energy, that no foreigner may ever rule over that soil, which contains the bones of our ancestors, and with which our most sacred and reverential recollections are associated.

The attention which the monuments of antiquity have already received, is therefore not without deep foundation. It is an omen that the Danish people, in their present advanced condition of improvement, will not seek to associate themselves with other nations; but rather, with looks turned to their native country, endeavour to combine the fervour and energy of the past, with the skill and ability of the present; and will, thus, maintain themselves free, and independent.

APPENDIX.

On the Examination of Barrows, and the Preservation of Antiquities.

In general, it is not to be desired that the ancient barrows belonging to the times of paganism, should be either opened, or removed. It is true they occur, in certain parts of the country, in such numbers as to offer serious impediments to agriculture; while they contain beside large masses of stone, which in many cases might be used with advantage. Still they deserve to be protected and preserved, in as great a number as possible. They are national memorials, which may be said to cover the ashes of our forefathers; and by this means constitute a national possession, which has been handed down for centuries, from race to race. Would we then unconcernedly destroy those venerable remains of ancient times, without any regard to our posterity? Would we disturb the peace of the dead, for the sake of some trifling gain?

Innumerable barrows have been destroyed by persons who believed that they should find great treasures in them. Experience however shews that objects of value are so rare, that scarcely one in a hundred contains an article of any worth. Such articles mostly lie under large stones, in sand-pits, or are otherwise concealed in the earth. For this purpose therefore, there is no inducement to open barrows. The only case which can render it desirable is, when the object is to gain information respecting the ancient history of our forefathers. But even investigations of this kind cannot always be regarded as desirable, they ought never to be undertaken from unseasonable or superficial curiosity; they should be carried on with care, and by persons of intelligence, who will know how to apply the objects discovered to the positive advantage of science. At the same time it is neither to be required, nor expected, that all or even the greater part of the barrows should, in future, be spared from destruction. On the other hand, it were much to be regretted, if the extension of agriculture should completely extirpate every trace of our ancient monuments. We cannot therefore refrain from recommending to patriotic individuals, to preserve at least those monuments, which are situated on heights, in woody districts, and in forests; in short, in spots where they scarcely offer any obstacle to the plough, or do not occupy land capable of being cultivated.

Under all circumstances, it is to be hoped that persons who are thus informed of the importance of these ancient memorials, will destroy no barrows, without paying attention to their structure, and the funereal objects which are deposited in them. A little care has often preserved important antiquities; and it cannot but afford gratification to every man, to assist in extending and improving our knowledge of the state of our country, and of our ancestors, in primeval times. With the view to promote and encourage this attention, we will endeavour to furnish a short guide to the barrows which it is desirable to examine, and to the manner in which their antiquities may be best preserved.

If a barrow must, of necessity, be removed, a complete description of its external form, its height, and circumference, should first be made. This description should explain whether it is surrounded, or enclosed, with large stones; whether chambers of stone are found in the middle of it; whether it has borne any peculiar name; whether any traditions are associated with it; and finally whether there are similar memorials in the same district, and what is their number. If the description were accompanied with drawings of the appearance of the barrow, it would naturally be an advantage. As it is of importance to know what is the internal condition of the barrow, and what may be the relation between the tomb itself, and the objects deposited within it, the tomb must now be examined with all possible precaution. If the barrow is one of the usual conical kind, it will be best to cut through it from south-east to north-west, with a trench of about eight feet broad, which, in more complete investigations may again be intersected by a similar trench, from south-west to north-east. It will often be sufficient so to excavate the barrow from the top, as to form a large round cavity as far as the bottom of the mound; which is always on a level with the surrounding field; for it is in the middle of this base, that the most important tombs are usually situated. In this proceeding it is, however, advisable to form a trench from the cavity in the middle, to the south-east side of the barrow, since tombs are often found here, and it might otherwise be extremely difficult to bring up the earth from the central cavity, when such cavity had obtained a depth of several feet.

As soon as the trench is begun, and the first covering of grass and heath is removed, we must examine whether vessels of clay with burnt bones and ashes, are not to be met with under such stones. These vessels, from their great antiquity, are so extremely fragile, that it is only with the greatest care they can be brought from the barrow in an uninjured state. When the surrounding stones are carefully removed, the best and safest mode of extracting the urns, is by introducing a board beneath them, then placing them in the open air, and after a few hours the clay becomes firm again. If the urn is uninjured, it is best to leave the burnt bones within it; among them at the top of the vessel are usually found some trifling objects which, however, are always worth preserving. If other curiosities are found near, or around such vessels of clay, as for instance small stone cists with burnt bones, and ashes, and the like, the excavation should be continued; and it will soon appear whether the barrow contains chambers of stone, or not. If the explorer meets with very large stones, which form the roof, or cover of a chamber of stone, he should follow the direction in which the stones are placed, in order to find the entrance to the chamber, which almost always faces the east, or south. It is by the entrance, in which corpses are not unfrequently deposited, that he must arrive at the chamber, which is always filled with loose earth, and a mixture of clay and pebbles. It is as the chamber is being carefully and thoroughly cleaned out, that the enquirer generally perceives how the corpses and antiquities have been deposited. Skeletons, and in particular sculls, must be preserved; and even the bones of those animals, which have been interred with the deceased may have a value for science. It must also be observed whether there is not a second stone chamber, in connection with the first. If, on the other hand, the barrow contains no stone chambers, the grave itself must always be sought at the base of the barrow, and this is usually surrounded by a stone cist, or covered with a heap of stones. In this case we must, on no account, remove the stones at once, because the objects in the grave might easily be injured by so doing. With the view to obtain space for the investigation, the best plan is to enlarge the cavity as much as possible, and to take off the cover of the tomb as soon as the earth which lies upon it has been wholly put aside.

It is generally considered of importance, in such excavations, that the cavities should not be made too narrow, in fact they ought to be very wide at the top, because it is always necessary to make them narrower in descending, with the view to prevent their falling in.

Finally, if it is a Cromlech, with one or more chambers of stone, the examination is rendered much more easy by clearing the chambers from the earth; in which operation one proceeds exactly the same as in excavating the chambers of stone, in the interior of the barrow. The earth surrounding the Cromlechs must also be examined, to ascertain if vessels of clay with burnt bones, and ashes, are to be discovered there. For all possible contingencies in excavating barrows, of course no exact rules can be laid down. But should there be discovered in a barrow, either chambers of stone, unusually large, or of wood, or any other remarkable objects, it will be advisable to discontinue the excavation, until the barrow can be examined by some intelligent person acquainted with the subject.

Barrows are the places where antiquities are most frequently discovered. But the digging of sandpits, the making of ditches, ploughing, and other labours of husbandry, are constantly bringing objects of antiquarian interest to light. By the removal of single stones, valuables have often been found at a moderate depth under the stones, which had been concealed there in ancient times. A few strokes of the spade where a large stone has formerly lain, may hence afford a rich prize. It has already been observed, that large stones should not be broken before they have been turned and examined, to ascertain whether they bear any inscription.

Next to the barrows, the peat bogs are the most important deposits of antiquities. The objects discovered in them have this advantage over those exhumed from the earth, that they are in a much better state of preservation. In bogs we may, for instance, expect to find stone-axes with the ancient handles of wood, while even bodies clothed, in their garments, have several times been met with in cutting through bogs. Hence it is doubly important to observe the greatest care in digging in the peat, as soon as anything remarkable is traced. The best mode is to dig cautiously round the spot, and to endeavour to extract all the objects it contains without injuring them. The mass of peat which surrounds them is not then to be removed immediately; for the earthy portions easily separate, when they have been somewhat dried in the air. At the same time, it is not expedient to dry all specimens in the sun, or in a strong heat, for articles which are not of stone, or of metal, are shrunk by this means. The relation of objects to each other deserves peculiar attention, and enquiries should be made whether more

are not to be found in the neighbourhood.   Whenever antiquities are traced, care should be taken to ascertain whether
similar objects occur in the surrounding district; for it has
been found that specimens of interest have been discovered
scarcely a step from the spot, where similar articles had been
found some years before.

Most antiquarian objects are covered with rust, or have otherwise lost their original appearance.   Articles of gold alone
are unchanged, because gold never rusts in the earth.   Silver
usually assumes a blackish tinge.   Bronze and copper in peat
bogs obtain a red or blackish tint; while in the earth they
usually become green.   Iron, of course, becomes very rusty indeed, except in the peat bogs.   Lead becomes oxydized; amber
acquires a resemblance to resin, by lying in the earth; glass
becomes covered with a thick coating and looks like mother
of pearl.   Bones are calcined, and become brown in the bogs,
where they are always best preserved.   Nevertheless, antiquities should never be cleaned, for they are injured by this
means, and so lose much of their value.   Still more should
we abstain from breaking them, which those who discover
them unfortunately often do, to ascertain whether they are
not of gold.

A very important rule is, that all antiquities, even those
which appear the most trivial and the most common, ought to
be preserved.   Trifles often afford important information,
when seen in connection with a large collection.   That they
are of common occurrence forms no objection; for historic
results can be deduced only from the comparison of numerous
cotemporary specimens.   In many instances, antiquities have
a value with reference to the spot in which they are found.
The law of Denmark provides that all gold, silver, and other
valuables, which are found in the earth, shall be forwarded to
the royal collections, and that the full value of the metal shall
be paid to the finder.   This arrangement, of course, does not
apply to objects of wood, stone, or clay; yet it is to be wished

that they should be sent to the national collection, where alone, in fact, they can prove of utility.

In Denmark, antiquities, respecting which parties are disposed to furnish information as to the spot where they have been found, as well as communications respecting the examination of barrows and other antiquities, should be sent to the Museum of Northern Antiquities at Copenhagen[a]. Objects of gold and silver, as already stated, are duly paid for by the authorities of the establishment; and if objects of other materials have been carefully treated and are of any rarity, the finder usually receives a suitable recompense, even if such objects are of no pecuniary value. A collection of antiquities has also been established at Kiel.

Parties who do not themselves possess any knowledge of antiquities, would do well, if they discover any thing remarkable to apply to the clergyman, schoolmaster, or other intelligent person on the spot, who may be able to determine what may be deserving of attention. In this respect it would

---

[a] In this country such objects should be forwarded either to the British Museum, where at length a department is to be especially devoted to the subject of our national antiquities, or to the Society of Antiquaries of London, whose Museum already contains numerous remains of very considerable interest. From the proper officers of the Museum or of the Society, persons sending antiquities will be sure to receive accurate information as to their nature and value.

While upon this subject, the editor trusts it may be permitted to him as a fellow of the Society of Antiquaries who has always taken a deep interest in the promotion of its Museum, and whose good fortune it was to be indirectly instrumental to the first attempt made to display the collection of antiquities in the Society's possession, to urge upon the fellows generally the propriety of following the example recently set them by Dr. Lee, who has most liberally deposited the beautiful series of antiquities brought by him from Ithaca, in the Museum of the Society. Indeed to all persons, who may have the good fortune to possess any remains of antiquarian interest,—more especially such as *illustrate the arts, manufactures, or social condition of this country* at any period of its history,—he would respectfully suggest that such objects lose half their interest and value when scattered in the keeping of individuals, and are only really profitable to the antiquarian student, when viewed in connection with similar objects. He would therefore beg to point out the Museum of the Society of Antiquaries as the place where the same might be most advantageously deposited.—T.

be of great utility if all over the country, in every large parish, for instance, or at least, in every district, several intelligent men would form an association, for protecting the most remarkable antiquities from destruction, and for co-operating with the lower classes, in examining barrows, and preserving antiquities.

OXFORD :
PRINTED BY I. SHRIMPTON.

ERRATA.

Page 20, line 23, *for* "The bodies were occasionally deposited in vessels" *read*
        "Beside the bodies were occasionally deposited vessels"

—— 21, line 19, *after* "had" *insert* "not"

—— 54, line 4, *for* "Ireland" *read* "Iceland"

—— 67, line 31, *for* "Amongst coins" &c., *read* "Of Roman coins from the third
        and fourth century we find few if any in Denmark"

—— 78, line 13, *for* "Thisled" *read* "Thisted"

—— 80, line 12, *for* "height" *read* "size"

—— 104, line 31, *for* "birds" *read* "beads."

—— 106, line 17, *for* "Holland" *read* "Halland"

—— 117, line 4, *for* "Gumer" *read* "Gwrmr"

—— 117, line 5, *for* "runu" *read* "kunu"

—— 118, line 30, *for* "kins" *read* "hins"

—— 127, line 29, *for* "vestiges and remains" *read* "few vestiges remaining"

—— 135, line 6, *dele* "nameless" *and for* "tribe" *read* "tribes"

—— 141, line 26, *for* "coins" *read* "course"

—— 147, line 12, *for* "South" *read* "North"

Printed in the United States
By Bookmasters